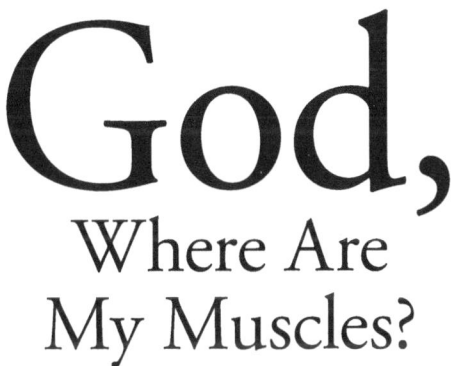

God,
Where Are
My Muscles?

God,
Where Are
My Muscles?

OSIANDER ROSE

ARPress
ILLUMINATING IDEAS.
EMPOWERING VOICES

ARPress
45 Dan Road Suite 5
Canton MA 02021

Hotline: 1(888) 821-0229
Fax: 1(508) 545-7580

Ordering Information:
Quantity sales. Special discounts are available on quantity purchases by corporations, associations, and others. For details, contact the publisher at the address above.

Printed in the United States of America.

ISBN-13:	Paperback	979-8-89389-083-9
	eBook	979-8-89389-084-6

Library of Congress Control Number: 2024909345

TABLE OF CONTENTS

GOD IS THERE

God will always see me through when I don't know what to do, He will place my head to rest

> When He knows I've done my best
> He will be there to comfort me
> He will be my eyes when I can't see
> He will be my ears when I can't hear
> He will be my strength when danger's near
> He will be my cushion when I fall
> He will hear my voice when I call

God will always walk me through
When I don't know what to do.

"And thou shalt be secure, because there is hope; yea, thou shalt dig about thee, and thou shalt take thy rest in safety."

Job 11:18

Other books by Osiander Rose

A World of Words Works vol. I, II, & III

The Usual Crowd

Preaching to the Tenth Pew What I Heard the Word Say to Me
Book 1: In the Early Years
Book 2: Coming Face to Face with God
Book 3: The Holy Ghost Will Guide You
Book 4: The Difference a Day Makes

The Seventh Pew Adventure:
A Boat in the Desert

Trials to Triumph

To order books from the author, please do one of the following:

Contact the publishing company directly
Call 217-351-4009/898-5496
Email yvosirose@yahoo.com

For Timothy Davel Rose; being small doesn't mean you can't be as good and strong as the big guy. God loves you and He will make sure you make it.

Love always mom ☺

Chapter One

The sunshine spilled through the window on a rather cold day in February 1968. A lady of fair complexion stood at the soda bar. She wore a khaki ankle length dress and high-heeled black boots. A black ribbon in her hair tied together to long neat braids. Theodore Newton Fieldwest saw her first and motioned for his friends to take a seat quickly, anywhere in the soda bar. Glass and Chime laughed at the young Newton. The lady stood almost two inches taller than him. Newton had always been a dare devil so he took on the challenge without a prompt from his friends.

"Hello young lady," said Newton making sure to show his perfect set of white teeth. They were his prize possession and the most attractive thing about him. He was always the shortest person in the crowd of the six-foot five inch boys he hung around but, he had perfectly straight white teeth. Today he was proud to have them. "How do you do?"

"How do you do," the lady returned politely.

"My name is Theodore Newton Fieldwest and what might your name be?" He didn't mind using his full name. He liked it.

He smiled waiting for her response.

"I am Caroline Adams. And I think I'm a bit too old for you." Caroline Adams started to turn and leave her space.

She took one step with her long slender legs before Newton spoke.

"Wait Ms. Adams. I only came over here to tell you that you are a beautiful lady and if you were my wife I would tell you that every day and I would make our children tell you the same thing." Newton was sure that's what he wanted to say. He felt like someone had said it for him.

"My, my Mr. Fieldwest. I'm sure you would. Well, I best get going now. If that was to happen, I'd expect to hear the word beautiful part your lips every morning."

The two of them laughed. Theodore bought the beautiful Caroline Adams two more sodas and they each went their separate way.

Newton returned to the table where Glass and Chime sat still laughing. Glass, whose real name is Jeffrey Harold, became friends with Newton only a couple of weeks after he and his family moved to Camden. Newton and Glass were in the same class from kindergarten to fifth grade. Glass' family moved to Philadelphia when he was in sixth grade and returned to Camden his freshman year of high school. Glass was given his name midway through his freshman year at Wheaton High School. He was caught peeking at the girls taking a shower after gym. The principal frightened him so badly that he broke the glass on the locker room door. Broken Glass was the original name and was shortened to Glass after a few months.

Chime, whose real name is Connelly McGranelly, lived in Camden his entire life. He and Newton became friends in preschool and stayed friends. Connelly is called Chime because he makes funny noises when he's nervous. He really chimes when he has to talk to girls. Newton and Glass always tease him about trying to propose to the woman he will eventually marry.

"Well Newton what did she say?"

"No, Glass what did he say to her? She was really smiling man. What did you say? And she's so tall. She's got to be six five." Chime was beaming. He knew he would have never approached such a beautiful lady as Caroline Adams.

"She's not from around here Newton." Glass turned to watch Caroline Adams slender long legs walk out of the door.

She walked gracefully to the parked cherry red '57 Chevy. "No not from around here. She's too pretty and well poised."

"And tall," Chime added.

"I told her that if she were my wife, I'd tell her every morning that she's beautiful and I'd have our children do the same."

Newton watched Caroline Adams hop into her car. The ankle length dress and her boots almost never hit the light snow on the streets of Camden, Pennsylvania.

"You didn't Newton, tell me you did though." Chime beamed again at the thought and bravery of Newton.

"I did man and I may never see that lovely woman again in my life!"

"For you Newton, I hope so."

"Do you really mean that Glass?"

"I really mean it and I promise I'll be at your wedding too. Promise man."

Newton, Glass, and Chime ordered two more sodas and decided to head for home. Newton was on a thirty-day leave from the military. He hadn't spent much time with his parents and his younger sister, Catheline Ann. His older sister, Clara Jean, lived alone. She didn't keep good company nor did she want company over. Newton was fine with it. He'd just call her a few times.

"Newton."

"Yeah Glass."

"How many more years are you going to serve?"

"I think two more and I'm done. I'm ready to have a family and stuff. I've spent almost ten years in the Army and I felt lonely about eight of those ten years. I may never get to play baseball again, but that's fine right now. I'd be too old anyway."

"You've done a good job and I sure hope your family thing turns out better than mine." Glass had a sadden look on his face. Four years ago, he thought he was getting the perfect lady.

She turned out to be the wicked witch of the west and the east.

The couple had been married for two years. Glass worked nights for six months and days for six months. It was his night rotation and he'd worked overtime one night. When he returned home early the next day, he found that his perfect wife, Shelby, had left him for the new mailman. Glass was devastated. Chime and Newton did everything to cheer him up but nothing seemed to work. Glass was nuts over Shelby. It took him almost a year to pull himself together. Friends like Chime and Newton were God sends at that moment in Glass' life. He vowed never to marry again.

"Me too Glass." Chime put his arm around Glass. Newton's arm followed.

"No matter what happens guys we will always be friends and we will always look after each other. It's so very important." Newton paused and looked directly at Glass and then at Chime. "Now if I marry Caroline Adams, you both had better be at my wedding."

"That's her name Newton? That's a gorgeous name." "She's a gorgeous woman," Chime added. "And when I see her again I'm going to tell her."

All of them laughed. They neared Newton's six-year-old beige pick-up truck. They drove off in the cold February night in 1968.

Two months passed by and the lovely Caroline Adams was back at the soda bar. Newton, Glass, and Chime came in an hour later. Again, Newton motioned for Chime and Glass to take a seat anywhere. Newton made his way back to the soda bar to talk with Caroline Adams. He wiped the sweat from his hands as he walked up to the bar. His heart jumped at the fact that he saw her again. He thought he'd never see her again.

This time Caroline Adams wore a knee length tan dress. She had on a darker shade of tan boots to match. The weather was warmer than in late February, hence the shorter skirt Newton thought. Her hair was pinned back neatly into a bun. No ribbon and braids this time. Newton could smell her perfume. His teeth sparkled. He stood near the six feet five inch beauty. His six feet made him appear much shorter but he didn't care.

"You are beautiful Ms. Caroline Adams."

Caroline laughed and was surprised he remembered her name and more so what he said in their last conversation.

"Why thank you Mr. Newton." Newton was happy to know she remembered his name. He looked up at the beautiful Caroline Adams.

"I told you I'd tell you that every morning and make sure our children said the same." Newton turned to see where Glass and Chime sat. He waved at them and they waved for him to bring the lady over. Newton worried about Chime and motioned that now wasn't a good time. Chime returned a gesture to mean that it was okay for the lady to come sit with them. Newton's heart raced. He was shocked to know that Chime would sit in the presence of a beautiful lady and not start chiming.

"My friends would like to meet you Ms. Caroline." "Oh please Mr. Newton, call be Caroline."

"I will if you'll call me Newton. By the way my name is Theodore Newton Fieldwest. And I think I told you this the last time we met. I'm telling you again just in case you want to pick the one you like best to call me by."

"You did and how thoughtful of providing me a choice."

"Anyway, my friends call me Newton. Nothing significant."

Newton led Caroline to the table in the corner of the soda bar.

Chime quickly made space for them. He and Glass stood to wait for Caroline to sit.

"Such gentlemen."

"Thanks Miss. My name is Glass and this here is my best friend Chime." Glass pointed to Chime who was beaming with happiness.

"Hello Miss. You are beautiful just like Newton said. You indeed are Miss." Chime didn't chime. He sat calmly and stared at Caroline for just a brief second. Newton was so proud of Chime but he would tell them after they left the soda bar.

The four of them drank three root beer sodas. Caroline told them she had to leave because her vacation was nearly over. They were right. She wasn't from around there. She was from Kansas City, Kansas. She had been here to visit her grandfather for a month. Newton and Caroline agreed to see each other when she returned the following winter for a visit to her grandfather. He promised he would try to get leave around the same time. They exchanged information and headed home.

Chime and Glass laughed again. They couldn't believe that a beautiful lady like Caroline Adams would notice an *almost* tall sparkled teeth stud like Newton. Her name alone bought sunshine to anywhere and anyone.

A year later in early February, Theodore Newton Fieldwest and Caroline Adams met in the soda bar. They were united in holy matrimony March 1, 1969. Glass and Chime were there as promised and as Newton had promised, he told Caroline every morning that she was beautiful. Even after the birth of their two sons, Theodore Newton Fieldwest continued to tell Caroline Fieldwest, the former Caroline Adams, that she was beautiful. Chime and Glass came to celebrate the birth of both sons. Glass was the godfather of Styles and Chime was the godfather of Boderrick.

Life for the Fieldwest family was grand.

Styles Regime Fieldwest was the first born. At age ten, he was still quite small for his age. He had scrawny muscles and dark smooth skin. He was virtually quiet but could get loud occasionally. He earned excellent grades in school and Mr. Fieldwest vowed to stay on Styles constantly because of his size and confidence level. Boderrick "Buddy" Newton Fieldwest was exactly like his father. Not much of a looker but he had all of his father's traits of a good talker. He had perfect white teeth at age eight. His confidence level ran laps around Styles. He was also as big as Styles, if not bigger. Nonetheless he had a lot of respect for Styles. He listened to him and he watched him. Mrs. Fieldwest worried a lot about both of the boys. She had different worries for the both of them. She worried that Styles would not grow and the children at school would tease him. She worried that Buddy would be so much taller and larger than Styles that the students would tease Styles more and Buddy would fight them to defend his big brother. Mr. Fieldwest tried to tell her that they would soon be men and her worrying wasn't necessary.

"They are like day and night Newton," he recalled her telling him. They were but they were all still very happy and all was well. They were really good boys.

"You are beautiful." Mr. Fieldwest stood in the frame of the kitchen door watching Mrs. Fieldwest scramble eggs for breakfast. She knew it was six thirty. For the past twelve years Mr. Fieldwest told her she was beautiful every morning at six thirty. He had his sons tell her the same thing before they each left for school. Mrs. Fieldwest smiled and continued her breakfast.

"Thanks Newton." Mrs. Fieldwest turned to watch Mr. Fieldwest take his seat at the front of the table. "Six thirty in the morning is the best part of my life. I can't believe that you kept that promise for twelve years. I love you so much."

"And you know I've always loved you."

"Mom are you picking us up today or is Dad?" Buddy grabbed a chair and waited impatiently for his breakfast.

Styles walked slowly into the kitchen and slid his chair out from under the table.

"Don't know yet."

"Mama?"

"Of course, I'll pick you up after school."

The Fieldwest family ate their breakfast. Buddy and Styles ran for the bus. Mr. Fieldwest left ten minutes later for work.

After serving twelve years in the Army, Mr. Fieldwest left the Army and decided to work for the government training young troops to become outstanding officers. He drove his 1979 Dodge pick-up to the University of Pennsylvania. It was almost 7:15. He liked to arrive at work early. He looked at his dress greens and headed toward his office. The day would be a long one. Mr. Fieldwest was extra happy because it was Wednesday. Scuds night.

The telephone rang.

"Yes sir." Mr. Fieldwest held the telephone receiver away from his ear.

"I will sir." The secretary poked her head in the door.

When she saw the receiver away from Mr. Fieldwest's ear, she quickly closed the door.

"That's a roger sir." He twisted the receiver in his hand. The final coordination for the Dining Out was pending. Colonel McCoo wanted Mr. Fieldwest to drive to New York for an emergency briefing.

"Out sir." Mr. Fieldwest returned the receiver to its cradle. He stared out of the window and turned the dial to complete his home telephone number.

"Hello." Mrs. Fieldwest tried not to sound out of breath. "Hello dear. I got a call from the Colonel."

"Colonel McCoo?"

"Yes dear, Colonel McCoo. He wants me to go to New York for the final coordination for the Dining Out. Are you and the boys going to be alright for a bit? I'll try to be home before dinner."

"Today's Wednesday you know."

"I know. Are you going to Scuds?"

"Don't know." Mrs. Fieldwest chuckled on the other end.

She knew her husband loved going to Scuds on Wednesdays.

That's not funny. But are you going to be fine?"

"We'll be fine honey. You go, be safe and hurry back."

"I will and will you please pick up the boys? They like getting home early and its Wednesday." He waited for her response.

"I will honey. Bye."

"Bye." The line went dead. Mr. Fieldwest rose from his desk and walked outside of the office.

"That was the Colonel I take it." Fredreda Washington made a funny face. It almost matched Mr. Fieldwest's.

"Yes, it was. I have to go to New York for the Dining Out final coordination. Are you going to be able to run things while I'm gone?" He watched Fredreda's face light up.

"Of course, sir. You be safe and we'll see each other in the morning."

Mr. Fieldwest grabbed his case and headed for the government issued van. It would take about two hours to get to New York. He was glad Colonel McCoo had made an early call. The traffic was clear. The driving would be a piece of cake.

Mr. Fieldwest pulled out of the university parking lot and turned on the radio.

* * * * *

"Where's Dad?" Styles had a funny look on his face. He placed his old backpack inside the car. Buddy made his way to the other passenger door.

"Thanks mom. I'm glad you came to pick us up." Styles made another funny face. This time it was to get Buddy's attention. He didn't want him to tell Mrs. Fieldwest that the Wallaces were still bothering them. He hoped to have the bullying problem solved by the end of the month.

The ride home was relaxing for the Fieldwest boys. Mrs. Fieldwest told jokes and promised they'd eat hamburgers and potato fries if their dad wasn't home by the time they finished their homework.

"We're going to go to Scuds without Dad?"

"Yes, and we'll order two hamburgers this time. It'll be great!"

Styles laughed really hard. He knew his dad loved Scuds' hamburgers. Every Wednesday after school they went to Scuds for hamburgers and potato fries. Sometimes Mr. Fieldwest ordered two. He told the boys they could only have one because they'd fall asleep before they got their homework done.

"Dad's not going to be happy mom." Buddy was laughing too.

"I know that's why we're going to do it."

"Mom rules," they both shouted from the window of the small car. Mrs. Fieldwest pulled up in front of the apartment.

The boys jumped out and ran inside to start on their homework.

Mr. Fieldwest didn't make it home in time to go to Scuds. The boys and Mrs. Fieldwest went. They each had two hamburgers and two orders of fries. At ten o'clock Mr. Fieldwest made it home to see his family asleep on the front couch. No signs of Scuds hamburger paper. It had been a long day for everyone.

CHAPTER TWO

The old alarm clock rang. It was very loud in the small empty room. Although it was the middle of May, Buddy felt cold underneath the thin warm blanket. He rose up on his elbows to check the time. Five-thirty. He still felt tired. He looked over to see Styles resting peacefully at age thirteen. Styles still looked like a small child. His four and a half-foot thin framed body lay motionless on the little bed. Even the rickety sounds from the bed didn't wake him. Buddy crawled over Styles to shut off the alarm clock. He then hustled to the bathroom to check. Still none. With a leak of disappointment on his face, Buddy returned to bed. He decided to finish the remaining fifteen minutes of sleep. In the fifteen minutes, he dreamt that God had given him huge muscles to fight off the Wallaces. He fought them off single handedly and Styles watched and cheered. When he got home, he and styles told their mom that the Wallaces were a problem but no more. No more. No more.

The alarm clock rang after the fifteen minutes of snooze. Buddy lifted himself from the bed. He knew it would be a long day at school and a painful walk to the babysitter's house. Hopefully not today because God would give him some muscles today.

"Buddy and Styles! Buddy and Styles," Mrs. Fieldwest yelled from the kitchen to the boys' bedroom. She forgot that there was no need to yell so loud. She was in an apartment, not their house on 75th Street. To keep from crying, she yelled once more before Buddy appeared in the small kitchen.

"Bu-"

"Hi Mom. You're beautiful this morning." Buddy stood near the chair where his dad always sat for breakfast. His mind wandered to a time when his dad said those very words.

"Hello Buddy. Isn't your mom beautiful?"

"He's only saying that because he promised me he would tell me that every morning if I married him. Funny thing Buddy, he kept his promise."

"That's my girl. Hey Buddy, come sit and have breakfast with me."

Buddy moved slowly and sat in the short chair next to his Dad. He could feel the warm love surrounding him as his mom handed both he and his dad a plate filled with grits and slices of bacon, a couple of sausages, two scrambled eggs, and a side order of toast. Mr. Fieldwest and Buddy sat and ate the delicious breakfast. Minutes late, Styles stepped into the kitchen. He was dressed but he still looked very tired. Styles ate quietly as Buddy ran to put his empty plate in the sink.

"Hey mom you're beautiful." Styles was excited to see his mother although he was tired from working through the night to get his project completed. He wanted an "A" on his project.

He would probably get it.

"Hey Dad, are you going to pick us up today?" The pause felt like eternity. Buddy hoped his dad would pick them up. The Wallaces were really starting to bother them more.

Buddy still hadn't gotten enough courage to tell his parents and Styles told him not to tell. After a while Buddy decided he wouldn't tell. Instead, he was waiting for God to give him some muscles to beat up the Wallace children. He and Styles went without lunch for the past month. Hershey and Conoga were just too big. They reminded each other to eat a good breakfast that would last until the end of the school day. Mrs. Fieldwest made sure of that and she didn't even know it.

"Yes Bud, I'll pick you guys up. I'll be there." Mr. Fieldwest grabbed his lunch from the counter, kissed his wife and left. The ride to the university was long. Mr. Fieldwest left later than usual and got stuck in the New Jersey morning traffic.

The usual parking place was taken. "I came too late." Mr. Fieldwest hastened his steps. He liked arriving early. It was the military discipline in him. He started the two-flight ascent on the stairs. Midway to the top of the first staircase, he clinched his chest. He was glad no one saw him this time. He promised to tell Caroline about it after he got home today. Today turned into tomorrow. Tomorrow turned into next week and so on and so forth. He never got it checked.

It had been several days and the pains came back. He still ignored the fact that he needed to see a doctor. He thought the sudden pains were due to stress and never talked about it to anyone.

One morning Fredreda and Mr. Fieldwest together took the two flights of stairs to their office. The sharp pain hit and Mr. Fieldwest fell to the steps. He tried to balance the fall to keep from falling on the fragile Mrs. Fredreda Washington.

"Newton you should get that checked. You really need to see a doctor." Fredreda had a worried look on her face. She flattened her skirt on her legs to stoop to help Mr. Fieldwest. She wiped his forehead and patted the pained area.

"Good thing it's early morning Mrs. Washington." "Newton this isn't the time to be formal. You need help and I'm worried. I'm really worried Newton." Fredreda decided against telling Mr. Fieldwest that she had seen him clutching his chest a few weeks ago. She decided to come in early and get some work done. It was Friday and she wanted to spend some each time with her family. She left a little after seven to get something out of her car. She was only been a few steps from the staircase when she saw him clutching his chest. Because of how men usually are, all macho and stuff, she watched from the top of the stairs. He didn't scream for help and he never said anything to her about it. So, she never said anything to him.

Today was different. She could see in his face that the pains were sharper. She sat next to him. She could hear his breathing slow down. She wanted to fix his uniform tie but decided it wouldn't look very professional on her part. The gold watch she wore on her small wrist chimed at 7:30. They had been on the stairs for fifteen minutes. A lot longer than the last time when she waited at the top of the staircase and said nothing. The length of time worried her more.

"I guess we needed that unauthorized fifteen minute break." She tried to smile but her heart worried that this was much more serious than they both wanted to believe.

"Promise me you won't tell Caroline." Mr. Fieldwest tried not to sound out of breath.

"I can't promise that Newton. I can't." Fredreda was almost in tears. She knew her voice rattled.

"Please. If she knew she'd worry."

"If she finds out later from you or that I knew and didn't tell, she'd be devastated at us both." Fredreda hoped her voice didn't echo too loud in the stairwell.

"I know I'm asking you to do the impossible, but I think it's just a little stress and I don't want my wife to worry. Please Mrs. Washington." Mr. Fieldwest rose slowly from the stairs.

"A fine time to try to be formal," she said to herself angrily and changed the subject quickly. "We had better get going.

Colonel McCoo may have called already and we're on the steps taking a break." They both strained a laugh. He looked up and down the stairwell to make sure no one saw him. They finished the rest of the stairs without a word to each other.

Mr. Fieldwest didn't get a call from Colonel McCoo. He was happy. He decided to leave early after thinking about his trouble on the stairs. He wanted to also surprise his boys at school. It wasn't Wednesday, but they'd like to see him anyway. He checked his closet. He must have taken his spare jeans home last week. He'd have to go in uniform.

"Fredreda."

"Yes sir," she responded as if nothing strange had taken place that day. "Yes sir, what can I do you for?" She stopped her work to look at Mr. Fieldwest.

"I'm fine Fredreda and please don't look at me like that." Mr. Fieldwest towered over her work desk.

"Is something wrong? You look different."

"I was glancing through the placements for next school year. I'm being moved to Halley High School."

"That's great. Styles wants to go to Halley when he graduates from grade school. So, we'll still get to see each other.

That's not too bad of a deal I hope." Mr. Fieldwest pressed the front of his uniform with both hands.

"You're leaving early, aren't you?" Fredreda changed her expression to a weak smile. She tried not to think of this morning. "Before you ask, you always do that when you're leaving early. I should know something about you after three years of seeing you every day." They laughed. This time it wasn't a strained one.

"You're great Fredreda and thanks for this morning." She could read the sincerity in his words and feel the force of the promise not to tell Mrs. Fieldwest in his tone.

"Promise me you'll get that chest thing checked Newton.

I'd hate you and myself if something happened to you.

"I will." He lied.

The drive home from the university to Camden was full of thought. Newton recalled the first time he suffered the sharp chest pains. It started about six months ago. So much was happening at the time. He didn't feel it was terribly necessary or the pains so severe that he needed to see a doctor or tell Caroline. The boys were growing so fast and he was very busy.

"Chime and Glass would have made me go see a doctor right away. They love Caroline," Newton spoke into the windshield.

"Dad, Dad," Styles yelled while running toward the car.

Mr. Fieldwest was so happy to see his boys he almost started crying. The boys were happy to see him because they were going to be crying after the Wallace children pushed them around.

"Thanks God," Buddy whispered on his way to the car. "Thanks."

The ride home was full of excitement. Styles made sure he reminded Buddy not to tell mom and dad about the Wallace children. The school year was almost over and they would be heading to a new school.

"That's great honey. I am so proud of you." Mrs. Fieldwest looked at Styles. "Are you going to be alright with that kid?" "Sure mom. Buddy is a bright kid. If he skips a grade and goes with me to Halley then I can still keep an eye on him." "Come here and give me a hug son. I am so proud of both of you. Styles you are such a man and I love you for it." The Fieldwest family dined, watched a little television, did homework, and went to bed. It was a good day.

"God, I sure hope the Wallaces don't go to Halley next year. That will be so horrible for us. Since I'm not going to get muscles from You at least You can send them to a new school. Amen." Buddy tried not to frown on his way to bed. He made a check mark on his calendar. Ten months of praying and not a muscle to frighten a roach could be seen protruding out of Buddy's skin. A tear fell on his pillow and sleep came fast.

* * * * *

14

The school year must have had wings. It was already the first week of June. Mr. Fieldwest had two more serious cases of chest pains and never told, the boys were still being harassed at school and never told, Mrs. Fieldwest thought all was going well, and Buddy still prayed for muscles to fight the Wallace children.

"Bear with me Buddy. We only have five more days of school and then we're on our way to Halley High. Both of us." The bus made its last turn.

"You're not mad that I'm going to be a freshman with you?"

"Why would I be? You're my only brother and we have to stick together. I'll just have to take extra classes to be a junior next instead of a sophomore."

"When I get my muscles from God then we'll be set. We can get good grades in high school, graduate with honors, and I'll be a professional baseball player and you'll be a –"

"A doctor Buddy. And what's this deal about muscles?" Styles gathered up his books and motioned for Buddy to get ready to get off the bus. He was sure Hershey, Conoga, or Monroe would be waiting to collect their lunch money.

"That." Buddy pointed to Hershey waiting outside by the curb. He saw Conoga and Monroe standing a few feet away. They were all there like clockwork. It was a pathetic situation for the Fieldwest boys. "When I get my muscles from God then I won't have to worry about Hershey, Conoga, or Monroe."

"That's crazy."

"Well what else can we do? What have we done even?"

"When did you ask God for your muscles Bud?"

"September."

"That's when they started picking on us."

"I know. I figured God is busy right now giving muscles to other kids and I'm next."

"We'll talk about that later. Did you eat a big breakfast, Bud?"

"Yep."

"Then we should be fine. Remember just give them the money and walk fast. Run if you have to." Buddy nodded and got off the bus. He wondered if Mr. Ples ever saw the Wallace children take their lunch money, why he never said anything to anyone? He must not have cared.

"God, I'm still waiting for my muscles," Buddy whispered as he stepped from the bus.

The three Wallace children came together like a well thought out plan. Buddy and Styles smoothly without breaking their stride handed over their lunch money.

"Now," Styles choked. Both boys started running into the school.

"Styles." "Yeah Bud."

"Did mom say she's coming to get us today?"

"I sure hope one of them does. I think Dad's coming. It's not Wednesday so maybe."

"Good."

"We'll be fine. You just keep praying for those muscles I guess." Styles patted Buddy on the back and they went into their class.

The next two days of school were horrible for Styles and Buddy but they managed and they never told their mom and dad the goings on at school every day.

The morning smell of breakfast woke the Fieldwest boys early.

"I'll race you to the kitchen Buddy." Styles made a big smile at Buddy. They were so happy to be on break.

"You're on big brother." Buddy and Styles headed for the stairs. Buddy stopped to check his posture in the mirror. "Well God, I guess you can take a break right now. We're almost off for the summer and I won't need those muscles right away.

But I'll need them by September because Styles and I are going to the same high school. See I'll skip eighth grade and start as a freshman with Styles. Isn't that cool. It's almost better than muscles." Buddy flexed and no muscles popped out. "Well God, he continued, "Take a break but please don't forget about me in September. I have a game today. We'll talk later." When Buddy realized he challenged Styles to a race to the kitchen he fled from the mirror. Styles was already seated with a forkful of eggs headed toward his mouth.

"Hey mom. You're beautiful. Now where's my breakfast girl!" Mrs. Fieldwest laughed and the boys laughed louder.

She just didn't know what a horrible year it had been for them.

"Where's Dad?"

"Work."

"This early? Does he know I have a baseball game and that it's important?"

"He knows and he'll be there."

The boys ate and Mrs. Fieldwest cleaned the kitchen.

The sound of the pick truck made the boys jump with excitement. Mr. Fieldwest had never missed any of Buddy's junior league games.

"Homework done?"

"YES SIR!"

"Well let's go!"

Four home runs.

"You're going to be a baseball star someday son and I'm going to attend all of your home and away games. You keep cracking that ball like that and you'll do well for yourself."

"And stay in those books too," Styles added.

The summer was fast approaching. Styles and Buddy were so excited. They didn't want to wish away the eight weeks of summer too fast. The start of the new school year would come all too soon. The boys didn't want to think about the continued harassment. Buddy kept thinking about getting his muscles from God.

That next day Mr. Fieldwest had one too many chest pain attacks. He had gone in but never told anyone. He had also given the nurse Fredreda Washington's name instead of Caroline Fieldwest. He instructed the nurse to only call Mrs. Washington first if there was an urgent situation. The nurse decided to call Mr. Fieldwest's former secretary, Mrs. Fredreda Washington, before placing a call to Mrs. Caroline Fieldwest.

Why he had requested it be done as such, she didn't know but she would ask. She knew his condition was more serious than he cared to hear.

"Why her," the nurse gave Mr. Fieldwest a puzzled look.

"Miss, I have had these severe chest pains for more than a year. I didn't tell my wife the seriousness of them. I'm afraid she already has too much to handle trying to raise two boys in the city of Camden. Times have been a little rugged for us both. My job schedule is terrible; I feel like my boys are holding something back from us and-" He paused to see the nurse staring at him. He knew the expression referred to the secret he'd kept from his wife for more than a year.

"Mr. Fieldwest, let me put it to you plainly and you can do with the information whatever you want. I truly wish your wife were here to hear this. But I can tell from your attitude that you'd rather she not. Very well. If you have a few more severe chest pains as you've experienced in the last two to three months it could be fatal. You have stressed your heart thus causing your lung capability to decrease. There's no need for you to be a war hero Mr. Fieldwest. You served your time. Nonetheless, you have to take care of yourself. First, bottom line up front, that job has got to go, Mr. Fieldwest. It's too stressful." The nurse went on and on reminding Mr. Fieldwest to take life easy.

"I will." Again, he lied.

He stayed on the job and accepted his promotion.

The school year was about over for Buddy and Styles. They were so excited to be going to Halley High School for their freshman year. Styles didn't feel terrible about he and Buddy being freshman together. His plan was to take extra classes and skip his sophomore year. Buddy didn't want to do any more skipping. He wanted to concentrate more on baseball during his summers.

Mr. Fieldwest was promoted to Colonel the last week of June. Only a few days after his promised visit to the doctor. He was excited to the point he'd forgotten about what the nurse told him about his job. He told everyone, who was also excited, that they would celebrate on Wednesday. The boys only had a few days left of school and they'd be able to stay out later. Everyone agreed. He promised he'd tell Mrs. Fieldwest after the little celebration.

Wednesday morning Mr. Fieldwest dressed for work as usual tried to ignore the throbbing in his chest. He was a soldier and was able to endure a lot of pain without public notice. He just hoped he didn't go down before he got out of the front door. He was sure to follow his schedule.

"Hey, you're beautiful." Six thirty in the morning Mrs. Fieldwest turned away from the stove to smile at him coming through the kitchen door. He hoped he didn't look flushed from sweating. He promised himself he'd go to the doctor tomorrow. "You need to quit that job Mr. Fieldwest. It's too much stress on your heart." The words faded from his mind as his plate of breakfast was placed in front of him.

"Did you see the boys on your way down?" They've been running late for school all week. Are we still going to celebrate your promotion today?"

"Of course." Mr. Fieldwest thought to himself, "Then I'll tell you or maybe we can go to the doctor together." Breakfast was delicious. Mr. Fieldwest kissed his wife and headed for the front door. Buddy and Styles ran to the front door to catch their dad leaving for work.

"Hey Dad," Buddy shouted from the doorway, "Are you going to pick us up today?"

"Of course, I'll pick you up today. Remember today's Wednesday and we have a celebration to celebrate!"

The next time Buddy saw Theodore Newton Fieldwest, he was in a cherry wood box in a small church on the corner of Mystery and Base. June never felt so cold. The tears rained from Styles' face. People always thought Buddy was the prize child. No one knew or saw the closeness Styles had with his father. The death of his father took him so sudden that he stopped talking. Wednesday, June 6, 1984. It was a Wednesday, two days before the end of the school year.

CHAPTER THREE

"What was that Buddy?" Mrs. Fieldwest continued cooking. "What did you say?" Buddy moved next to Mrs. Fieldwest. "Mom you are beautiful." Mrs. Fieldwest felt the tears on her cheeks. Buddy didn't notice because he'd already taken his seat next to the empty chair. Styles had not joined him yet. Buddy was a little worried but he didn't go back to the small bedroom to fetch him.

"Are you ready to eat my child?" Mrs. Fieldwest tried to sound motherly, but her voice shook terribly. Buddy noticed and decided not to say anything. Grits, bacon, sausage, and toast. Deja vu.

"I won't be able to pick up you and Styles today, Buddy. I need for you two to walk to Aunt Clara Jean's after school. Mama's got to work late at the clinic.

"Mom."

"Please, not this morning, Buddy. Just eat your breakfast before it gets cold." Buddy knew Mrs. Fieldwest was crying.

Before he could speak again, Styles walked in. It had been almost a year and Styles had not grown an inch. He's slender, dark brown frame stood in the kitchen doorway. The entire house grew silent all of a sudden.

"You're not picking us up today, mom? Buddy and Styles waited for a response. Instead, Mrs. Fieldwest fled from the kitchen, leaving Buddy and Styles to eat breakfast alone.

"Everything has to be alright soon. Please God." Buddy frowned as he repeated the thought in his head. Styles washed the morning dishes and they headed out to the bus stop.

"Styles." Styles looked. Buddy stood a few inches taller, but his very young face showed concern. "Styles. Today is Friday and I'm afraid. Everybody fights on Friday." Buddy waited for an answer, a puff, a grunt, something connected to bravery. Styles did his slow methodic shuffle to the school bus. Mr. Ples, the retired Command Sergeant Major, yelled at the boys. Buddy picked up his speed. Styles continued his shuffle.

"You better pick up your dry face and bring it to this bus boy!" Mr. Ples had sweat bubbles dripping from his forehead although it was rather cold. Buddy thought about how Dad used to rush them to the car every morning when they were much younger so that they weren't late for school. It was fun but…

"We're coming Dad. We're coming!" Buddy was practically dragging Styles. Buddy wore his new jeans and shirt. It was a good day. Buddy hit five home runs at his championship game. The family was going to celebrate. The crispy jeans moved quickly as Buddy pulled Styles arm trying not to break a sweat.

The heat from the maroon seat on the Dodge '57 found its way to Mr. Fieldwest's new gray dress shirt.

"Come on boys!" His voice was heavy. He had not intended to break much of a sweat. "My boy is going to be a star!"

"A professional Newton." Mrs. Fieldwest sat on the passenger's side of the Dodge. She smiled happily as the boys came toward the car.

"A star, a professional, whichever. He's going to play ball and he's going to play well and I'm going to be there to see it all!" Mrs. Fieldwest turned to wipe Mr. Fieldwest's forehead as the Dodge pulled away from the small house. The roaring of the old engine bought Buddy back to reality.

"Thank you, Mr. Ples. It's just that…"

"Aw boy, go take a seat. Next time you late I'm going to have you get down and give me some. Right here." Mr. Ples pointed to the aisle of the school bus. Buddy smiled and took his seat. He figured Mr. Ples was old in age and didn't remember that his dad had passed on. Styles shuffled to the back of the bus. Buddy tried to stay brave but he knew Styles was worried about the walk to Aunt Clara Jean's. Before the death of Mr. Fieldwest, Styles wasn't really afraid of the Wallaces. They irritated him, but he was never really afraid. He made sure Buddy didn't try to stand up against the three of them. He knew the Wallaces frustrated Buddy. He had always been bigger than Styles but not big enough to handle Hershey, Conoga and Monroe. Monroe was having a change of heart because she started to like

Styles. In a way, that could've been sort of an advantage for them. Styles never told Buddy. He figured he wouldn't understand.

"You just wait for those muscles from God. They're coming. You just wait." Styles would say that to Buddy when he would get really frustrated about Hershey, Conoga and Monroe harassing them daily and no one knew or did anything. "You just wait for those muscles from God. They're coming."

"Hurry please." Buddy felt tears forming behind his eyes. He had to hold them back, for Styles' sake. One Friday Hershey threatened to really put some hurting on Buddy Monday morning. Styles was more frightened because he wasn't talking. Buddy was disappointed because God hadn't given him muscles yet. They didn't go to school. Buddy prayed everyday for his muscles. On the following days they hoped Mrs. Fieldwest didn't come early because they weren't there. She never did. Although he knew his mom and dad would have been very upset at report card time, he figured she'd feel better when she realized that they weren't seriously hurt. He at least hoped they would. It was a risky week, but it made them both feel better. When the report cards came out, Styles kindly wrote a letter to Mrs. Fieldwest explaining away the five absences. Mrs. Fieldwest never checked into it. Styles told Buddy he had to keep his grades up so that there was no reason for their mom to come to the school inquiring. Buddy agreed.

"We're not going to school today Styles. We can't. Hershey said he's going to put a hurting on you. He ain't kidding. We're not in grade school anymore brother. And what's worse is it's Friday!" Styles didn't speak a word but he shot a glare at Buddy that could cut. "I'm sorry. I didn't mean it like that. I mean that we're older and they've always been older. I think Hershey and Conoga should have been graduated from high school. But what do they do? They hang around Halley when they should be at Jacksonville somewhere with their faces in a book. And we have to run to Aunt Clara Jean's house every time mom has to work overtime and she barely has time to pick us up from school so that we don't have to run. The only benefit we're getting, well at least I'm getting is that I can run the bases to home faster." Styles watched Buddy's lips move. He knew that Buddy was ready to explode. He still didn't speak but Buddy knew he was not in agreement of skipping school. Buddy wanted to hang out in the park behind the clubhouse. They'd do their work and read until an hour before school dismissal time. That would give them a peaceful walk to Aunt Clara Jean's.

Maybe it wasn't such a good idea not to tell that they were being bullied terribly everyday for a couple of years and it continued even in high school. Now Dad would never know that people were hurting us, Buddy thought.

"God I really need those muscles before I start college. Where are they?" Buddy hoped he didn't sound like a nuisance.

The rugged school bus pulled to the front entrance of the two-story building. The students exited. This morning Buddy decided to search for the Wallace crew. They enjoyed a fresh night, which bought on fresh thoughts. Maybe not good ones, but at least they were new ones. A few seconds of searching resulted in the Wallace crew standing in superior mode on the back fence of the playground. Hershey, the oldest of the crew, looked to have a new scar on his face. He stood 5 feet 6 inches at about age 16. He could easily pass for 20. Buddy was told that he'd gotten into a few clubs. Impressive. Hershey made an ugly face when his eyes met Buddy's. He never noticed their features from grade school. Perhaps due to the fact that Styles always made them run after handing over the lunch money. Today Buddy got a better look. Styles stood near Buddy who could feel his skin crawling. Conoga, the survivor of a set of twins, was terrorizing another student for his lunch money. The dark thin shirt complimented Conoga's blue jeans but not his attitude. Monroe, the youngest of the crew, stood next to Hershey. Her tightly braided hair didn't stop her from grinning from ear to ear when she saw Styles get off the bus, "She would whip him in a heartbeat but now she's smiling at the very sight of him." Buddy spoke loud enough for Styles to hear him. He just cut a stare. "I already know Styles and I won't tell anyone. It'll all come out in the wash sooner or later. I just wonder if sooner is better than later."

The school day was long and worrisome. Buddy thought hard about a way to dodge the Wallace crew after school. He was tired of years of running and months without muscles. He wondered if maybe God just didn't want him to have them. Maybe because baseball players don't really need them. "I do, but not for baseball," Buddy prayed sadly.

Mrs. Fieldwest made it clear that they were to walk to the sitter's house. She didn't and couldn't understand the fear that accompanied going to school for the Fieldwest boys. Buddy tried to concentrate on Language Arts and a plan of escape. The escape plan got the better of him.

"Buddy, how did she feel?" Mrs. Trontoner did not repeat her question. She stood squarely over Buddy. Sweat poured inside his skin. He hadn't heard any of the question and he knew Mrs. Trontoner would not repeat it. Buddy had to think fast. He was an advanced freshman in high school. His brother Styles was down the hall. The death of their father didn't make matters better. If he would be sent to the office, the secretary would call his mom. If they called his mom, they would probably take liberty to tell her tell her about last Friday. Then they would go on and ask her about the five- day absence. The buzzing in Buddy's ears startled him. Mrs. Trontoner stood in place.

"Are you all right Buddy?"

Buddy looked to Mrs. Trontoner. "You'd never understand."

It slipped out! It slipped! Buddy's sweat poured from the inside out. He tried in much desperation to recapture the tone of the response. His head was so clouded he couldn't even remember his response. Mrs. Trontoner did not repeat her question or Buddy's statement. The pastel-colored dress made Buddy dizzy. He was so worried about the after-school affairs that he was ready to risk getting a detention for the afternoon.

Styles wouldn't want to wait for him. Mother would be terribly upset. Dad was no longer around to help.

"Buddy." There was what seemed like an eternal pause.

"I'll see you at lunch." Buddy breathed a sigh of relief.

"I don't know which one I want more, my dad back or my muscles. God which ever one is easier for you."

At the end of the school day, Hershey and Conoga pushed and shoved Buddy and Styles all the way to their aunt's house.

Buddy ran a little and dragged Styles when they almost got to the gate where the big dog barked. At first he frightened Buddy. Styles jumped a little too. They ran but had to stop short of Aunt Clara Jean's else she would ask why were they running.

They stepped into the dark house. Buddy went to the kitchen. Styles went to the bedroom.

* * * * *

"Not going to class. But I am going to wait for the Fieldwest boys today." Hershey made his ugly face. He made no attempts to pull up his sagging jeans. "They are such wimps. And they been wimps since grade school. Now Buddy and Styles are in the same grade. I don't know them that well so who's the dummy?" He drew another puff from his cigarette. Monroe reached for it and was lightly slapped on the hand by Conoga. Monroe turned her face and sat upright on the picnic table.

"How much more time we got boys?" Monroe didn't want to see Styles get beat up by Monroe and Hershey. She patted her coarse braid and just sat. Monroe had grown to like Styles since eighth grade. She never really let on to her brothers because they'd tease her. Styles was still short and small for his age. Buddy was passing him up. She had heard about their father but she never really knew her own so she couldn't relate. Hershey or Conoga said the time.

Hershey, also a twin, has a few other half siblings scattered about the city and maybe the state. He doesn't know where the twin is and now believes there is no twin. At age 14, he is still upset with not knowing his father. He and Conoga have been together since birth but the other siblings have spent very little time with them, visiting once or twice a year. In third grade, Hershey was tested. His scores were very low. His mom told him that the teacher recommended he take special classes. If his grades didn't improve, he'd have to attend a special school. Conoga, on the other hand, was born a genius. He was promoted to third grade after completing his first grade year. He did everything he could to help Hershey get through the school year. It was very hard work. Then Monronisha was born. The Wallace mother had to get another job to support the extra bundle of surprise. Hershey wasn't doing well in school so he dropped out to sell drugs to help pay some of the monthly bills. Ms. Wallace quickly used the money to pay the bills.

She was so caught up in her two jobs and caring for the new baby that she had not bothered to figure out where the extra hundreds of dollars a week was coming from. After a life-threatening phone call one Sunday morning at two, Ms. Wallace got up from her rickety bed. She went straight to the boys' room. They weren't there. Little Monroe lay in her crib sleeping peacefully. Ms. Wallace felt her head tighten. She hated to wake her sleeping baby. Five minutes later Ms. Wallace and little Monronisha were driving up and down the streets of the dark neighborhood. Eight blocks from the apartment complex stood Hershey and Conoga making a dangerous transaction. Ms. Wallace decided to wait in the car. She thought about some of the episodes from television. She thought about how she ruined her own young life to spite her parents. It wasn't worth what she was seeing right before her eyes. She sat under the streetlight and prayed.

The minutes seemed like hours. The transaction was completed. Hershey and Conoga walked quickly toward the direction of the car. They didn't see their mother's car parked on the empty streets. As they were about to pass, Ms. Wallace cracked the passenger window and called politely for the boys.

"Hershey and Conoga." Ms. Wallace said in a trembling voice. "Come here right now." The words were tight. She fought back the tears. She had let both boys' father take advantage of her success. She would have been a star performing in California by now. She was stubborn and stupid. "Calm down Teresa Wallace. It's not their fault. Just calm down." The boys moved quickly in a frantic and tossed themselves into the car. It was cold inside of the car. Ms. Wallace silently drove the eight blocks home. Something had to change. This was all too much to digest at a little after two o'clock in the morning.

Hershey and Conoga were made to promise not to make any more transactions. They didn't. Instead, Hershey dropped out of school. He hung around the house and here and there. When he turned sixteen, he got a job to help Ms. Wallace with bills. Conoga and Monronisha skipped school on certain days to spend time with their brother. That situation went on for a little while. Then the children met the Fieldwest boys and the trouble started and continued.

"2:15. One hour 'til dunes." Hershey rose from the bench and threw the cigarette butt in the small waste can. Monroe was nervous. She was missing her math test and she didn't want Styles to get jumped again. Through the years, Styles' sense of importance perhaps rubbed off on Monroe. She was always able to earn good grades, when she went to class. She secretly kept Styles as her role model. She wanted to be like him and she liked him. It was a weird feeling. A feeling her brothers would never understand. The current situation with her brothers, the bullying, and Styles gave her a feeling of being torn between love for her brothers and the love for Styles. Buddy was somewhere in the mix because he's Styles brother. Nonetheless, Monroe knew she couldn't betray her brothers and she wondered if Styles would ever forgive her for letting them continue bullying them every day. She vowed to do a makeup test Monday, get a perfect score, and show it to Styles when her brothers weren't around her.

"To the babysitter's. To the babysitter's." Conoga teased Buddy and Styles as they took the short but long walk from school to their aunt's house. Aunt Clara Jean's was four blocks from the Wallaces' apartment complex. Everyday for four weeks, Buddy and Styles passed the big German Shepard on the way to Aunt Clara Jean's. The dark blue-black creature barked heavily on the porch. Buddy got a better look at the dog one day when he and Styles thought they were going to have a worry-free walk to their dad's sister's house. Mrs. Fieldwest had to work late every night for two weeks. It was terrible.

Today Buddy decided if the Wallace children caught up to them, to go in the gate where the big dog stood on the top step barking heavily. No sooner he made that decision, he heard Hershey's voice. Buddy held his breath and headed quickly for the low iron gate. The German shepherd barked in a frantic. Styles kept in stride with Buddy.

"How much more harm can this dog do? Hershey and Conoga are going to beat us blind anyway and God forgot I needed my muscles to fight them." Buddy walked toward the gate pretending he had reached Clara Jean's house. Styles slowly followed.

A "You know Buddy you may just be right." look came across Styles' face. He was more afraid the Wallace boys were getting closer than he thought.

The big blue-black German shepherd appeared to be less dangerous than Hershey who picked up his step at the sight of them going for the gate. Styles knew Buddy was trying to fool them into thinking that was Clara Jean's house. For a moment he was confused but immediately oriented himself when he saw the dog. The German shepherd lowered his bark as Buddy and Styles stepped inside the gate. Buddy wished he had some left-over lunch to give the big dog. Styles stood in one spot shaking. He looked over his shoulder to see that Hershey and Conoga slowed their pace. Monroe smiled weakly in Styles' direction. Styles did not return a smile. How could she act like she likes me and then at the same time make my life miserable thought Styles to himself. He almost asked God for some muscles too but left that prayer to Buddy.

The Wallace children appeared to be talking among themselves. They were trying to figure out whether or not to go inside the gate. They couldn't remember seeing the big dog and the dog was too big to take a ridiculous risk like Buddy and Styles had.

"Now we know who the dummy is," Hershey teased from down the street. Monroe smiled again in Styles' direction and again no smile was returned. Buddy's presence silenced the dog's bark when he stepped inside the gate. Styles stood closer to the gate watching the Wallace boys and Monroe. Buddy walked up the stairs toward the big dog. The boys were in luck. The big dog sat still. Hershey, Conoga and Monroe waited for a while then went the opposite direction.

"Thanks dog, you really saved us this time." The big dog let Buddy pet his head.

"What's your name dog? We may need you again." Buddy rubbed the dog's neck. The big dog let out a happy bark. Buddy looked around the porch. No one came outside to check on the dog. Surely someone would want to know why the dog was barking so much and so loud. No one came. Buddy checked the dog's collar. He found none. He rubbed the big dog around his neck and petted him again on the head. "I'll just call you, let me think." Buddy watched Styles relax.

He watched the Wallace children walk across the street in the direction of Baly's Corner Store. He turned to watch Buddy talk to the German shepherd.

"Safety. You like that?" Buddy whispered in the dog's ear and stroked his fur. He gave the dog a hug. Styles motioned for Buddy to come on. It was getting late and it was all too obvious that Styles didn't want to worry Aunt Clara Jean. They walked quickly to get to Aunt Clara Jean's four blocks up the street. It was the first time in a long while that Styles picked up his pace. It was an even longer time since Hershey and Conoga didn't complete their mission of chasing them practically to the front gate of Aunt Clara Jean's home.

"Thank You, God," Buddy whispered as he closed the gate to Safety.

"Hello babies. Are y'all hungry? Auntie made some sandwiches and soup for an after-school snack."

"You mean lunch for us because we didn't have any again today." Aunt Clara Jean turned to ask Buddy what he said. "Oh, I'm just mumbling Aunt Clara Jean. Don't mind me." Styles resumed his normal pace as he walked into the house.

The front room was dark and unhappy looking. The darkness mixed with the furniture didn't compliment Aunt Clara Jean's smile and personality. Buddy shook as he walked through the dark room. The kitchen was illuminated and smelled of homemade soup. Buddy suddenly felt hungry. He looked around for Styles. He had stopped in the bedroom. He sat limp in the old chair in the corner. He looked tired and worried. Buddy made a mental note to check on him before Mrs. Fieldwest came to get them. He returned to the kitchen to have some soup and sandwiches with his aunt.

"How's school baby?" "Good"

"How are your grades?" "Fine."

"Where's your brother?"

"Sleep." Buddy didn't like that he could only answer Aunt Clara Jean with one word. It didn't seem to bother her. She continued to ask questions.

"How's your mom?" "Fine."

"Is Styles coming around?"

"No." Buddy knew what Aunt Clara Jean meant.

Aunt Clara Jean didn't give up. She asked more questions while she searched for bowls, spoons, and cups around the kitchen. Buddy watched her and thought about Safety.

"God, please stay with us. We, me and Styles and mom, really, really need you. And of course, I still need those muscles."

CHAPTER FOUR

It had been almost two years since the death of Theodore Fieldwest. Six feet, two hundred thirty-five pounds of solid muscle, and very strong in heart as well as physical strength lay six feet under in Lincoln Cemetery. Theodore Newton Fieldwest was a remarkable man during his time. Excellent son, outstanding soldier, dedicated friend, devoted husband, and caring father. The pastor spoke the words over Theodore Newton Fieldwest as they lowered the cherry wood casket into the ground. The words played over and over in Styles' mind. He recalled crying so hard the day he and Buddy and his mom came home from the funeral. Nobody heard him except God. Styles loved his father with all of his heart. He was so angry that he left them here to fight the Wallace children and watch their mom struggle everyday to make sure food stayed on the table. He vowed to do whatever it took to be so successful that his mother would never have to work again. He had to get himself together to watch over Buddy. Buddy wanted those muscles so bad, but Styles thought they needed more than just muscles. They needed a miracle.

Theodore Newton Fieldwest played professional baseball in Birmingham, Alabama before being drafted into the Army. He played the position short stop and hit a record of homeruns. The fans loved him. Although at the beginning of the season he was mistreated by the white fans he never gave up. He went all over the world playing baseball. Many of the southern states did not welcome him. People of the north accepted him but the games had to be short. Mr. Fieldwest feared his life and that of his family after returning from a Michigan trip. By the start of his third contracted year, he received papers to report to South Korea. He knew then that he wouldn't return to the game. While overseas, his commander handed him the Georgia Times. He was first pick for the Atlanta Braves.

He was so excited. The media didn't even know he was called to serve the country.

"We'll hold a spot for you Newton. You come see us when you get out."

Three years passed. Then five years flew by. The rank increased and the job toughened. Eight years in and Newton had a chance to visit home.

The Army was demanding. Newton served twelve years in the service and was too old to play professional baseball by the end of his term. Sometimes he felt that the military cheated him out of his career, but the day he laid eyes on Caroline Adams made him change his mind. He had almost forgotten about baseball until the birth of his second son, Broderick. The dream of baseball flooded him like magic when Boderrick was two years old. Father and both sons were playing kid ball in the yard. Buddy threw the ball so far it surprised Newton. He grabbed the bat and had him take a few swings. The ball went sailing!

"Son, you're going to be a star baseball player just like your dad! You just wait!" Mr. Fieldwest jumped up and down. Mrs. Fieldwest laughed. "He's so young still, Theodore. But I believe you." It was a happy moment.

Mrs. Fieldwest checked her watch. Two more hours to quitting time. She would pick up her boys and head home. It was Wednesday. She tried not to think about Scuds hamburgers. It was difficult and she was tried. The tears began to roll down her face. She pulled a tissue from her pocket. She realized she'd been crying most of the day. Walking toward the sign-in desk, Mrs. Fieldwest took another moment to reminisce.

"You're beautiful." Mr. Fieldwest whispered to his wife. He rubbed her chocolate shoulder length hair. The curls fell four by four in place. "You're beautiful." He hugged her and she returned it with a greater grip. Neither knew it was the last time they would see each other like this. The kiss was wet with love and sincerity.

"Have a good day dear."

The sign in desk was cluttered as usual with memorandums, newspaper clippings and dust.

The door closed. Mrs. Fieldwest finished the dishes and set out the meat for dinner. She checked the clock and called the boys down to catch their school bus. She watched them race for the school bus. It was sort of fun to watch them race out of the house with only seconds to catch Mr. Ples. Mr. Fieldwest left only minutes before the boys.

"I forgot to ask Dad to pick us up today Styles." Buddy trotted and clutched his backpack on his shoulders.

"He'll be there honey. It's Wednesday."

Buddy was anxious to eat. I must be growing because breakfast isn't holding me as well, he thought. He jumped from the kitchen table and ran down the narrow hall to the small bathroom. He raised his shirt and checked himself in the mirror. He frowned at his scrawny reflection in the mirror. "Never mind God. I know you're too busy." Buddy peeked in on Styles who sat staring in the ceiling. I better eat. I don't want to starve waiting for my muscles. His plate was already set by the time he got back to the kitchen. Aunt Clara Jean wasn't in the kitchen. Buddy was relieved. He could almost feel tears forming and he didn't want to have to explain anything to Aunt Clara Jean that would take more than one word. He bit into his sandwich and blew his soup to cool it.

Trying not to think of past times, the memories crept up on him.

"Mama, do we have to go to school today?" Styles' eyes lit with excitement. It was his last year of grade school. He was extremely happy. His soft light brown eyes danced in his head. The blue jeans weren't new, but the new T-shirt went well with them anyway.

"You're going to get that Afro trimmed. Styles, I want you to look like a man for graduation luncheon." Mrs. Fieldwest escorted the boys out the front door.

"What about me too mom?"

"Oh, baby we almost forgot. You're graduating too. I'm so proud of both of you."

"You're beautiful mom and I love you." Styles pulled Buddy gently by his left hand. He brushed Buddy's hair with his hands. Buddy wasn't big for a seventh grader. Styles was just small for an eighth grader. Buddy wore a light green sweater and a pair of Styles' old dress pants that were getting to be too small. It was rather cool for a sunny Tuesday in the middle of May. Buddy's hazel eyes appeared coal black. He was smiling to see Styles in such a great mood. He loved Styles dearly. He was his big brother.

"But Mom he has a little less than two months." Buddy let Styles pull him. "Aren't you graduating in June, Styles?"

"Yes, Buddy and so are you."

Come on the bus will be here soon. Buddy and Styles waved to Mrs. Fieldwest as they reached the corner to turn.

Leaving early this morning gave them time to talk to each other. Mr. Ples would still yell and rush but at least it was a good morning start.

"I'm going to start getting up early to see Dad before he leaves."

"Me too." Buddy walked swiftly alongside Styles. They were at the bus stop.

"Come on boy." Mr. Ples wore his army jacket. He smiled energetically as Styles and Buddy loaded the bus.

"Hello Mr. Ples." Styles smiled and guided Buddy onto the bus and to the third seat from the front.

"Morning to ya Styles. How's your Daddy boy?"

"He's fine Mr. Ples. I was just telling Buddy here that I'm going to start getting up early to see Dad off."

"Yeah, your pa's a hard worker boy. I have so much respect for him." Styles and Buddy took their seats. The bus pulled away from the curb. Styles took out his history book and began to read chapter six, Abraham Lincoln and the Abolition of Slavery. After reading about two paragraphs, he nudged Buddy. Buddy took out his novel and began reading.

Two months before, Styles told Buddy that he needed to do more recreational and nonfiction reading. At the end of Buddy's sixth grade year his reading performance dropped drastically. Styles thought it was primarily due to the Wallace children bothering them every day. Styles made a pack with Buddy. If he bought his grades up, he would ask mom to take them both with her on take your child to work day the following year. Styles got to go with Mrs. Fieldwest to his dad's job that year because he kept good grades. Buddy agreed. His grades were improving then they dropped.

"Stay focused Buddy. Don't let Hershey and them ruin you."

"I won't Styles. Promise." Buddy kept that promise. He improved so much that his scores allowed him a chance to graduate from grade school a year early.

"I've read almost this whole book Styles."

"That's good Buddy. I want you to go with me on take your child to work day. You're my baby brother. Plus, Dad will love to see you at his job so he can brag about you and your baseball skills. We'll have fun." Styles smiled and turned back to his book.

The boys read for the forty-minute ride to Ritz Grade School.

The bus made a clean turn and parked in front of the big, chimney red school. Mr. Ples waited for exactly thirty seconds before opening the door and another fifteen seconds before signaling the students to exit. Styles and Buddy placed their books inside their book bags and got off the bus.

The principal stood on the last step of the second level of stairs. The pin striped navy-blue suit fit snug on his shoulders and belly. Mr. Newet was the principal of Ritz Grade School and had been for eight years. He was very familiar with the Fieldwest boys for they had been students of Ritz since kindergarten. His sliver hair blew very lightly as the students sped past him into the building. Styles spoke softly to Buddy on the way up the second level of stairs. "You have a good day Buddy. I'll meet you here after school. And Buddy, don't worry about the Wallaces. We'll survive some kind of way." Styles smiled at Buddy and they split the top level going their own direction.

* * * * *

Aunt Clara Jean startled Buddy. He spilled a little soup on the table. He looked around for Styles who was probably still in the small room sleeping. Buddy hadn't seen him actually do homework but he was sure he had. One thing Styles didn't want was a permanent life in Camden, New Jersey.

Buddy continued to eat his lunch. He sipped the soup, which he found to be rather delicious. Aunt Clara Jean took quick bites from the sandwich. She glanced at Buddy every now and then. She could see the fatigue in his eyes. She missed the happy, loud laughter indicating after school fun that accompanied them on each visit. That was before the death of Theodore. She never understood why Caroline always called him Newton. She couldn't remember if her mother had named him Theodore Newton or Newton Theodore or just Theodore. Newton must have been a nickname. She wouldn't have known. She was so much older than Newton and times were very different then. The children gave themselves a name to fit their personality. Theodore or Newton, she loved him just the same. It really hurt her to see the children so sad.

She rose from the table. Buddy moved slightly but didn't look up from his bowl of soup. Aunt Clara Jean walked thoughtlessly from the kitchen. She had only on her mind the slurping sound of Buddy eating his soup. She walked the short path to the front room. Styles lay limp on the guest's bed. His thin frame looked sunken and drained. Although Aunt Clara Jean couldn't see his face she could feel the heat of suffering from Styles small body. She was certain that the passing away of Theodore Newton Fieldwest played the greater role in Styles' sudden withdrawal. She softly thanked God for watching over the boys.

"They are doing so well Lord. Please stay with them. Please help them through this." She blew a kiss to Styles. She returned to the kitchen to see Buddy helping himself to another sandwich and bowl of soup.

Styles lay dreaming hard. The entire ordeal devastated him. The more he thought about it the more he hurt. He knew Mrs. Fieldwest was on her way to get them. Another day at Halley High School was getting to be too much for him and certainly Buddy. He forced himself to go on for Buddy especially.

The doorbell rang. He could hear his mom's voice. She was tired he could tell by the change in her tiny voice. He lifted himself from the bed and headed out the door. He waved at his aunt and looked for Buddy. Buddy looked down the street to see if he could at least hear or see Safety. He heard nothing.

CHAPTER FIVE

"Mom, do we have to walk to Aunt Clara Jean's after school? We could ride the bus here. Styles is responsible and we're both old enough to do either. I'm a sophomore and Styles might as well be a senior at the rate he's going. Aunt Clara Jean is getting to be a ripe old age you know." Buddy chuckled at his own humor. He had heard his father use the phrase when he spoke of his grandmother and great aunts. It just seemed to fit perfectly into the present conversation. The chuckling died out quickly and the thoughts of Theodore Newton Fieldwest surrounded the two of them. Mrs. Fieldwest's smile was fading. Buddy knew he didn't want to walk home and risk being bothered by the Wallace children. Yesterday was terrible but the strange thing about it was Safety. Safety was the one who scared off Hershey. Buddy felt good. "If I walk home or ride the bus home, I won't see Safety anymore." Buddy pretended to agree that they should continue to walk to Aunt Clara Jean's after school. Styles wasn't around to argue either way. Even he wanted to argue, what would he say. He wouldn't even talk. One more day of the Wallaces for now wasn't as near the time already past.

Mrs. Fieldwest secured a promotion at work. That meant more overtime. She was already scheduled to work over time for the next two weeks.

2:15 came too fast for Styles. He wrapped up his fear and headed out the front doors of Halley High School. He counted down the days to the end of school. Styles couldn't believe that almost three years had passed and the Wallace children still chased them! He decided to do summer school and not even return the following year. He thought about Buddy. If Buddy got his muscles this year, then he would be all right without him. Again, Styles almost prayed for God to please hurry but he knew that that prayer was between God and Buddy. He also tried not to be angry with God for taking his father and for taking so long to help him and Buddy.

He waited for Buddy at the designated spot. He watched for Hershey or Conoga or Monroe to suddenly appear and start pushing him or teasing Buddy for being taller or something of that nature. Buddy walked up and they began the walk to Aunt Clara Jean's. Buddy almost hoped for the Wallace children to show their faces. He dare not tell Styles.

Bingo! There they were right where they always waited. Styles noticed that Monroe was dressed like a real girl. Of course, she'd be. She was growing. He still didn't smile. He thought perhaps he would've had she been alone. He took a little time to notice her short red skirt and tight blue top. She wore sandals! Not much of a fight was going to take place from her. Buddy never noticed. He was sizing up the boys. They looked like grown men. Fit. Maybe they had his muscles. Styles thought for the moment that God had finally come through for him. God had given Buddy his muscles. Styles almost leaped with joy but noticed that Buddy was no bigger than he was when he saw him at lunchtime.

"To the babysitter's house girls. You got to go to the babysitter's house girls. I can't believe you ladies can't go home alone and you're almost in college!" Hershey teased and poked at Styles who just kept walking. Buddy tried hard to hold in his anger. "Don't you ever do what they do especially if it ain't good." The words of his father burned his ears but he kept his cool.

Buddy's heart jumped when they were steps away from the gate where he met Safety some almost three yesterday. "Come on Styles, we might as well go in and get bit by the dog. At least he knows why he's biting us. Hershey and Conoga can't even tell us why they've spent half their childhood bothering us." He was sure to speak loud enough for the Wallace children to hear him. Styles didn't talk but he did follow Buddy. There stood Safety at the top of the stairs barking heavily. His bark could be heard across town but still no one came to the door and told him to shut up. Strange. It had all been so strange. Buddy reached for the gate just as Hershey was going for another push on Styles. Styles nearly ran inside the gate. Safety stopped barking. Hershey, on a dare, followed Styles and Buddy inside the gate. Safety barked and jumped at Hershey who ran out of the gate. Styles saw Monroe laughing and stopped immediately when

Hershey looked at her. She turned and smiled at Styles as they walked across the street again in the direction of Baly's Corner Store.

Buddy patted Safety on the head and rubbed his neck. "I sure wish I had some food for you Safety and I'm really glad you remembered us. Thanks for your help. We better get going before Aunt Clara Jean calls my mom. One Saturday I'll come by here and spend some time with you. I don't think I have a game this week." Buddy looked at Styles who motioned for him to get going. Time had been wasted running from Hershey but things looked a bit promising with Safety. Buddy waved at the big German shepherd.

"Aunt Clara Jean," Buddy paused. He wanted to be certain not to hurt her feelings. He understood she was old so he paused before he spoke again.

"Have you ever heard a huge dog barking in your neighborhood? Have you at least seen one?"

"No, not that I recall. This is primarily an old folk's neighborhood son. We are too old to take care of big dogs Buddy."

Buddy couldn't say more. It would be too many words. Styles wasn't talking much and he really didn't know how to talk to Aunt Clara Jean. He definitely would if he could, but he couldn't. He changed the subject. "Aunt Clara Jean, can I watch television in the front room? Styles is exhausted. I'll be done with my homework and stuff by the time mom gets of work." Buddy prepared to pick up his meal hoping Aunt Clara Jean would allow him to watch television in the front room.

Styles came in and went straight to the bedroom. Buddy was certain he'd do his homework. He dare not go and ask him. He was the younger child. He watched the little fifteen year old walk slowly into the room. He turned to give Buddy a strange look. Buddy froze. Styles had the same look. It was the very same look.

* * * * *

The principal's office was a long journey for Styles.

Suddenly the school that always felt cramped and crowded seemed quiet and empty. The sound of Mrs. Stems' voice over the intercom was tight and cold. Styles knew there was something wrong. The beautiful, gentle voice the students were used to hearing each morning came over the loud speaker as basically "Styles, I got bad news for you".

"Mr. Casey?" Mrs. Stems stuttered and struggled for words. "I have been trained to stay calm. I can't do this,"

said Mrs. Stems in a whisper. "Mr. Casey, is Styles Fieldwest in class right now?" Styles repeated the stuttering words as he walked to the principal's office. He shivered in the warm empty halls. It wasn't passing time, which gave Styles more time to think about the strange voice of Mrs. Stems coming over the loud speaker.

"Yes, as a matter of fact he is?" Mr. Casey adjusted his tie.

The silence made him speak. "Can I help you Mrs. Stems?"

The students all felt the tightness of Mrs. Stems' voice. They sat quietly.

"Mr. Casey, can you please send Styles Fieldwest to the principal's office. Thank you."

Click.

The sound of the intercom switch was like a second signal to remain silent. They did.

Styles moved slowly from his seat. He was glad he had already read the pages for Napoleon III. He asked Peterson to take notes for him. He straightened up his books. Mr. Casey didn't say anything. He just motioned for Styles to leave.

He looked around a few times to see if Buddy had been called as well. There was no Buddy.

"I guess mom isn't picking us up early. That's a good sign. I really need to be here for my language test." Styles picked up his pace. In the dark hallway, he saw a figure similar to his mother. He slowed his pace and tried to focus on the figure as he slowly moved toward the figure, the figure moved at the same pace toward him. Styles heart pounded and it made his ears hurt. When Styles saw the figure was Mrs. Fieldwest, his eyes filled with tears. Mrs. Fieldwest never made surprise visits and she would let Styles know ahead of time that she was coming. Styles was in eighth grade and his mom kept that promise for years. She never came to the school for surprise visits and she never failed to tell him that she would be there, and to act right while she was there.

The tears filled his eyes quickly to replace those already fallen. Mrs. Fieldwest embraced Styles. They hugged each other in the empty hall. Passing time would be in ten minutes.

Styles tried not to cry out loud this time. He put his face in Aunt Clara Jean's pillow. He cried silently. The pain was still there.

CHAPTER SIX

It was a beautiful Saturday in May. There was no baseball game this Saturday. Buddy jumped up but was surprised at first that there was no smell of bacon. He knew then that the reason was because his mom was tired. The week was so full of excitement, hard work, and strange stuff. Buddy threw off the sheets. He saw Styles still in bed and decided not to wake him. He had a hard week too. He spoke to Aunt Clara Jean for the first time in as long as Buddy could remember.

"I think he's the muscles Buddy's been praying for since sixth grade."

"Styles!" Aunt Clara Jean held her heart. Styles knew Buddy heard her. Seconds later Buddy came tripping into the front room. He stumbled on the rug at the door.

"Is everything all right Aunt Clara Jean?" I thought I heard a shout." Buddy's heart was racing. He couldn't bare another tragedy. Aunt Clara Jean stood there pointing at Styles. Buddy looked at Styles as if to ask what's wrong with him. He didn't get it.

"I was just," Styles' eyes began to fill with tears. It had been a long week. Styles couldn't handle the harassment from Hershey and Conoga while debating whether or not to talk to Monroe. Safety was the best thing that happened to Buddy since the death of their father. Buddy hadn't noticed that Safety was his muscles from God. Every time he walked in the gate Safety stopped barking and Hershey and Conoga and Monroe left them alone. It was like the dog was hypnotizing them to go across the street to the corner store. It was simply amazing and Buddy hadn't noticed yet. Styles had hoped Buddy would've noticed after the first year but he never did. He let Buddy continue to pray for muscles although their morning confrontations and after school beatings from Hershey and Conoga were less. Monroe spent more time idling in the back than throwing any punches or smarting off at him and Buddy. It could be due to the fact that the children don't half go to school anyway or because the principal stands on the premise almost every morning. But that had never stopped them before. Nonetheless it lifted some worry off Styles and Buddy still hadn't noticed the number of times Hershey wasn't there when they got off the bus.

Styles continued trying not to burst into tears. He remembered the time he and Buddy walked to Aunt Clara Jean's. It was all the same routine. They picked up the pace while Hershey and Conoga, with Monroe trailing, attempted to close the gap.

Buddy and Styles headed straight for the gate of Safety. It was no longer a rush for them to get inside the gate but rather a relief. Buddy would sit next to Safety and pet his head, rub his neck and try to offer him a little food. He enjoyed the petting but never ate the food. After several attempts over a period of time, Buddy stopped trying to give food to Safety. Styles stood near the steps and watched Buddy. "This dog must be Buddy's muscles. Hershey never bothers us when we're inside this gate," Styles thought to himself as he watched Buddy one afternoon.

"Thanks so much Safety. I feel safe when I'm around you. I think about you all the time and I always look forward to seeing you every day." Buddy petted and rubbed Safety.

"Styles, why is there no dog bowl around anywhere?" Styles didn't answer. He shrugged his shoulders and watched Hershey, Conoga and Monroe head across the street to Baly's Corner Store.

Hershey and Conoga pretended to look for something to buy. They had Monroe stand outside watching Buddy. She watched Styles prance back and forth inside the gate.

Styles blocked her view of Buddy and the dog. That's what she'd tell her brothers. Hershey would run out of the store demanding the details of what she observed.

"They left right after you two went inside," Monroe would say. As she finished her thought, Conoga and Hershey came out of the store.

"Where's the dog? Who came and got the dog?" Hershey realized he was shouting at Monroe. His mom would slap him if she found out. Monroe stayed calm because she knew all she had to do was tell and Hershey would be in big trouble.

"I don't know," she said. "And I really don't care," she added in a whisper.

"I don't get it Hershey. That huge dog stands on the top step everyday and barks like crazy. Then those two losers walk in the gate and like magic the dog stops barking. We get to the gate and before we even touch it, that dog jumps at us. We get frightened and walk over here to pretend again like we're buying something. We can't buy anything because we don't have money." Conoga knew he was frustrated and near a shout but something wasn't coming together. Conoga looked at Monroe who looked at Hershey. Hershey rubbed his head and stared across the street.

"So…where'd you say the dog went Monroe?"

"No, Hershey, where's the lunch money you took from those dummies?" Conoga stared at Hershey. He could feel the desperation in his voice. He didn't have the money. He didn't want to answer Conoga's question. He was too afraid to say he'd lost the lunch money every day since the day Buddy and Styles stepped into that gate. Sure, they were taking it from them as usual but by the end of the day the money was gone. "But where?" Hershey was sure to keep that question to himself.

"Something isn't right boys," Monroe said while gazing across the street again. She honestly didn't see the dog. She couldn't remember if it was because she was too focused on Styles or was what she saw really what she saw. It was weird. Yes, Hershey lost the money but he didn't want Conoga and Monroe to know and he hoped Styles and Buddy never found out.

"I sure hope I'm not losing my head guys," said Conoga. "You're not man. Just hang in there. We'll get those knuckleheads," Hershey replied.

"That I'd like to see," added Monroe.

"I just think that Safety is Buddy's muscles. I really do?" Buddy sat next to Aunt Clara Jean on the antique couch. "What do you mean Styles? I don't get it. Why does Buddy need muscles from God?" Styles didn't know where to begin and Buddy didn't know whether to run from the room to miss the embarrassment or stay and listen to Styles voice and logic. Mom didn't even know yet. He stayed. Styles tried not to direct his thoughts of the conversation with his mother when she was at her threshold of grief and needed a release. It was important that they understood where he was going with this conversation. It had been long time since Styles spoke more than ten words. It was a revelation for Aunt Clara Jean and Buddy. They sat not saying a word.

* * * * *

It was on a Wednesday. Wednesdays started becoming their worst day of the week. Buddy had a special baseball practice for a big Saturday game. The apartment was quiet and lonely even though Styles and Mrs. Fieldwest were still there.

"Styles can I talk to you while Buddy is at practice?" Mrs. Fieldwest was tired from the long week. She requested the day off to be with her sons. Although she didn't realize Buddy had practice, she was glad to see Styles walking around the house. She knew he wasn't going to talk so she came to him instead. She gently grabbed his arm and escorted him to the couch. He looked about the room as if he was seeing it for the first time. Mrs. Fieldwest didn't pressure him to talk or look directly at her. She began slowly talking about the day she went to the school. As horrid as it was to repeat in words or actions, she felt like she had to tell someone. Who better than her son, Styles, who could understand her grief?

"Yes ma'am, I understand."

"Please Salley. Please call me Caroline. I'm trying to be strong and you're not helping."

"I'm sorry Mrs. Fieldwest. It's just that…"

"Oh Salley, I didn't mean to snap at you. I'm sorry, I just can't stop crying."

"If it makes you feel better." Mrs. Stems paused and looked around the office. She saw the other employees busy at work.

"Caroline," her voice was just above a whisper. Mrs. Fieldwest knew that Mrs. Stems didn't like getting too personal on her job. Mrs. Fieldwest wiped her tears and tried to consider the position she put Mrs. Stems.

"I just need for Styles to come to the office. I'll be there shortly." Mrs. Fieldwest played with the dishcloth. She looked around the kitchen. It appeared to be in fairly good shape.

She leaned to take a second look in the family room. Tears shed.

"Caroline?"

"Yes Salley." She could tell Mrs. Fieldwest was not in the best good mood to talk right now.

"Caroline, what's the problem? Are you okay? Has something happened to Newton?" Salley stopped, but it was too late. She hoped the next question wasn't why. Newton's doctor called her a few weeks ago concerned about his health.

She wanted to know why she was to be called first if something happened instead of his wife. When the call came in, she was on break. She didn't return the call because she was scared.

Salley held her breath. This was not a good time to hash out personal issues. She held the phone hoping Mrs. Fieldwest didn't ask. Not knowing what else to say or where to take the conversation, Salley asked, "Is Mr. Fieldwest at home now?"

The line went dead.

Mrs. Fieldwest slapped down the receiver. Her attitude stirred. "What was that all about," she asked herself. "Now is not a good time for this Caroline. But, why had she called him Newton? What happened to Mr. Fieldwest? Everyone else called him Theodore. Except for his really good friends." She paced the kitchen. Not Mrs. Stems. She and her husband were like sister and brother and now just wasn't a good time to pass judgement. She felt stupid and immature. Mrs. Fieldwest wanted to cry. She'd go to the school and speak to Styles. Not Buddy. He was too young. She also made a mental note to apologize to Mrs. Stems. It wasn't her fault.

Mrs. Fieldwest checked the clock. She would use five minutes to tidy up the family room. She checked the entire house then headed to Ritz Grade School. She rehearsed over and over what she would say. She promised not to get swampy-eyed when she saw Styles.

Styles always liked Mrs. Stems. He wondered why his mom was upset about her asking his whereabouts. Maybe she knew for a long time that Dad wasn't well. He hoped she continued without him verbally prompting her. He stared out a window until he heard her inhale. She was ready to continue. Her voice was low and cracked at the first word.

The drive to the large school was as probably as long as Styles' walk to the principal's office. The afternoon traffic moved at a slow, boring pace. Mrs. Fieldwest checked her make-up and blouse. She had taken very little time to take care of her clothing and more time trying to put the family room back in place.

Six minutes later Mrs. Fieldwest pulled into the visitor's parking lot. Again, she checked her make-up. She slowly stepped out of the old Dodge '57. She knew Mr. Fieldwest loved that car. Her long legs met a ray of sun as she closed the door. The dull maroon car had no glistening marks from the sun until she moved away heading to the front steps. She felt strange. Inside the big school looked so empty because there were no children filing up and down the hallways. There were no children running up and down the two flights of stairs. There was no Mr. Newet standing on the top step of the second level in a snug fitting pin striped suit. No silver hair blowing as the children went past. "I hope I can do this. God give me strength." Mrs. Fieldwest thought back on her last visit to Ritz. It was in August of the year when she registered the boys. Mr. Fieldwest had come too.

This time Styles fought back his tears. He needed to be strong for his mom. This wasn't a good time for him to cry. The tears rushed to his eyes. He fought hard to keep his face dry. Styles hoped his mom didn't hear his deep breathing. But he knew she knew. She recaptured what happened.

"This is my last year at Ritz mom and Dad. I'm excited."

"I am too son." Mr. Fieldwest gave Styles a warm hug.

They walked arm in arm up the two levels of stairs. Mrs. Fieldwest and Buddy walked closely behind. Reunion T-shirt and a pair of blue jeans for the boys and Mr. Fieldwest, and Mrs. Fieldwest wore a long blue jean skirt. She smiled at her family. It was a beautiful day in August.

"I hope I get Mr. Casey for history and Mrs. Figgle for math.

I want to do well because I want to go to Halley's Technical Prep next year."

"You'll get there." With his left hand, Mr. Fieldwest pressed the front of his shirt, dragging his hands down to his jeans.

He didn't want to release the arm in arm hold with Styles.

"This is Kodak moment," said Mr. Fieldwest. He could feel Styles' excitement.

"Mom do you think I could go to Halley's too?" Buddy chimed.
"Sure honey."
"Buddy, I'll make sure you get there. We'll work together."
Styles smiled at Buddy.

Styles was happy to know he got Mr. Casey for history and Mrs. Figgle for math. Buddy was also satisfied with his schedule and teachers. The Fieldwest family left Ritz and went to Apple Cider for brunch.

Styles didn't know what to say. He didn't want to let his mom know that the Wallace children harassed them every day. Every day since Buddy was in sixth grade. He couldn't recall how or why it all came about and he never forgot that it never ended. He didn't want to tell her that he made Buddy work extra hard so that he had a chance to skip a grade. He didn't want to tell her that he just had nothing else to say since the sudden death of his dad. Life was terrible, but he tried to keep an opened mind that things would get better. He watched his mom's lips quiver. She was as beautiful as his dad said. She was sad but she was still beautiful. He remembered laughing out loud and really long when his dad told him how they met and what he promised to say every day. Six thirty in the morning and Wednesdays were once the best times of his life. Now they were the hardest times for him. They were like nightmares. He knew he had to be strong.

"God, where are my muscles?"

Mrs. Fieldwest tackled the second set of stairs. It wasn't passing time. She moved in a half-hurried pace to get to the Main Office before the bell rang. She stopped in the girls' restroom to do one last check before signing in at the front desk of the Main Office.

"Hello Mrs. Fieldwest." Mrs. Stems wore a colorful dress. Mrs. Fieldwest couldn't see if it was long or short because she stood behind the waist high counter. She was pleasant trying to hide her grief. She tried to portray anything that resembled a warm welcoming smile. She could see the worry in Mrs. Stem's eyes. This was not the time she reminded herself.

"Hello Salley." Mrs. Fieldwest knew that she should've said Mrs. Stems or Salley or not use a name at all. A simple payback. How childish, she thought, but it felt good at the time.

"I'll be with you in just a moment." Mrs. Stems pretended to be busy with paper work. She wanted to prepare herself. She didn't know the purpose of the visit and she felt she needed a few minutes to prepare herself for the news.

"I wonder what happened. It couldn't be too bad. She looks well." She shuffled the papers. Then she pretended to write notes. She looked up and motioned Mrs. Fieldwest into the empty conference room. The two ladies tried to leave the tense feeling in the office. "Oh Salley, I do apologize for earlier. I don't know where to start and I'm tired. Where should I begin?" Mrs. Stems pulled out a chair for each of them.

"I'm not upset, it's just that I take my job very-"

"I understand. Did you call Styles to the office yet?" "No, I decided to wait for you to tell me more information. I didn't want to jump to conclusions." Mrs. Stems fiddled with the tail end of the colored dress. Mrs. Fieldwest noticed it was quarter length.

"That's a very pretty dress," she commented as she fished for words.

"Thanks," she said politely.

"Salley, I understand your position and I apologize. It's just that this morning Newton and I had a great conversation. We talked about Styles and Buddy's progress in school. It was a beautiful morning as it always is for us. He hadn't complained necessarily, but he made mention of chest pains and slight headaches for the last couple of days. I said it was stress.

Basically, I talked him out of going to the doctor. See today is Wednesday and he got a promotion and we were all going to go out to celebrate and-" Mrs. Fieldwest choked up. Mrs. Stems waited for Mrs. Fieldwest to gather herself. Fredreda told her about Newton's sudden chest attacks. She never told Mrs. Fieldwest because she promised Fredreda she would say nothing. She tried not to make obvious expressions of shock.

She stayed calm letting Mrs. Fieldwest continue.

"Well, the doctor's office called me this morning. Newton was rushed to the emergency room from work. I was too shaken to go. I nearly destroyed every room in the house except the kitchen. Then I called you. I was so snappy. This day has been hard and trying for me. I just want to speak to Styles before they get home. I don't want them to get home and find out their father is in the hospital and I don't know what'll happen next. Styles will talk to Buddy. I know he'll do a better job than I will."

The ladies sat in the conference room. Mrs. Stems was speechless. Mrs. Fieldwest felt like she had not said enough and said too much. Mrs. Stems checked the antique clock hanging on the North wall. Twenty-five minutes until passing time. She wished she'd never made that promise to Fredreda, but now was not the time to discuss it. She knew it would hurt her later. She knew before now that Mr. Fieldwest needed to see a doctor. She prayed for the best situation.

She needed to get more information from Mrs. Fieldwest before passing time. She swallowed hard and took a deep breath.

"Caroline what did the doctor say?" Mrs. Stems felt like the temperature in the conference room dropped. The warm June day suddenly felt like the middle of January. Her ears rang and her throat ached.

"Is he?" She couldn't finish the sentence. She watched Mrs. Fieldwest, who had left her seat, walk toward the conference room window. Mrs. Stems went to call Styles to the office before passing time. She pressed her colorful dress as she rose from her seat. She wanted to ask Mrs. Fieldwest if she would be fine but decided against it. The space was already tense and cold. She left the room in a hurry. She was relieved to find the Main Office quiet and calm. She checked her files for Styles' schedule.

"She wants to talk to Styles, not Buddy." Mrs. Stems located Styles' schedule. "Mr. Casey, history. He loves that class." The principal and assistant secretary weren't in the office. She was, in a way, glad to be there alone. Mrs. Fieldwest was still in the conference room. Mrs. Stems wished she could call Fredreda. She better not. She was worried about speaking over the intercom as well. She wanted to walk to Mr. Casey's class and finger Styles out. She feared she'd breakdown on the way. Theodore Newton Fieldwest was a lovely man. He was well liked by many. Mrs. Washington adored him in a sisterly way and so did she. It was difficult to explain especially to Caroline at a time like this. She took two deep breaths, fumbled for the buttons on the intercom, and spoke.

The tears were falling fast. Styles didn't know what to do. It was more like he couldn't do it. He wanted to fetch her a tissue from the bathroom but his legs wouldn't let him move. He wanted to gather her into a warm secure embrace but he felt it would be awkward and he was too young. He held back his own tears and watched her cry like a baby. She cried the same as he when he was on the small bed at Aunt Clara Jean's house. He didn't know which was worse him watching her cry or the grief of the tragedy that stabbed him over and over and over. When she got control of her emotions, she felt pressed to finish the story.

* * * * *

"Mom, I think the bell is going to ring. Where's Buddy?"

Styles remembered clearly asking his mom about Buddy. He and Buddy were close. They did everything together.

Mrs. Fieldwest couldn't remember how she came out of the conference room. She couldn't remember what she said to Salley. She didn't want to hug Styles too hard or too long.

Her eyes filled as they walked the rest of the way to the Main Office. Styles was glad to be out of the hallway before the bell rang. Mrs. Fieldwest escorted Styles to the conference room.

She hadn't noticed if Salley was at her desk. The door of the conference room closed slowly behind them. Mrs. Stems returned to her seat, as the "click" of the conference door broke the silence in the Main Office.

"Mom, is something wrong? Please don't make this a long drawn out lecture. Just tell me straight out if something ugly bad has happened. Where's Buddy? You never come to the school in the middle of the day. Please mom." Styles whispered in a pleading voice. He didn't know what to say really. Just his mom being there was a shock. Maybe she found out that Hershey and Conoga bullied them every day. Maybe Buddy finally broke and told her he hasn't had lunch at school in like forever. Maybe she found out that one week they didn't go to school at all. Maybe she wanted to know why Buddy was praying for muscles. Or, maybe he had gotten them! Styles list grew in his mind as he watched his mom try to form the words for her next sentence.

Styles looked older than twelve years old. She looked him up and down. She was proud of him and could see at that very moment how Buddy was developing into a younger version of Styles. Bigger and taller, but the same personality. She promised herself to be a brave woman about this. She juggled backwards and forwards in her head the conversation with Dr. DeVito.

"I'm calling about my husband."

"His name?" The crisp yet pleasant voice made it difficult for Mrs. Fieldwest to sound professional. She could hear the cracking in her voice. She must not have responded because the crisp voice repeated the question.

"Can I have his name please?" The voice asked in a crisp tone.

"Newton Fieldwest. Theodore Newton Fieldwest." Mrs. Fieldwest was startled to hear her own voice.

"Identification number?"

"I don't understand."

"Are you and your husband covered?"

"Yes. Health Alliance." Mrs. Fieldwest volunteered the name of the provider anticipating the next question.

"Pardon me?"

"The insurance company is Health Alliance."

"Thank you. Do you have a person number or a policy number he uses?" The crisp voice waited for the numbers.

Mrs. Fieldwest could imagine the medium height, medium frame woman sitting at her office chair. Her shoulder length, blonde hair was probably pulled back in a bun so that she gave a professional appearance. She imagined the woman in a short dark blue two-piece suit. She had her forms in position waiting for the person number.

Mrs. Fieldwest fumbled with the receiver. She intentionally made the call in the kitchen so that she could recite her husband's person number. She couldn't understand why she didn't go to the hospital. Fear? Guilt? At the moment, she was afraid and didn't feel any guilt. Nonetheless, she should have gone.

"I couldn't. I just couldn't, I just couldn't," Mrs. Fieldwest repeated.

"Pardon me?"

"Oh no. I wasn't speaking to you."

"Could you hold please?" The crisp voice disappeared.

Mrs. Fieldwest cried a little. She just couldn't understand why she hadn't gone to the hospital? Why she hadn't demanded Newton go see the doctor? He wasn't even old. He'd turned thirty-four just last Spring.

She switched mental gears while on hold. She thought about the birthday surprise.

Styles moved closer to Mrs. Fieldwest. He put his weak arm across her back. He knew Buddy would be home soon and he didn't want him to see mom like this. Mrs. Fieldwest dwelt on the birthday surprise. She tricked Mr. Fieldwest into taking her and the boys to dinner. She pretended she'd forgotten that it was his birthday. The plan was to reveal the surprise at dinnertime.

Mr. Fieldwest left early from work to pick up his sons. "Hey Dad."

"Hey Dad." Buddy and Styles were glad to see him. Hershey and Conoga were positioning themselves to push and tug Buddy and Styles after the playground cleared a little. When the boys saw their dad, they were so excited. Styles was glad Hershey hadn't touched him in front of his dad. There would have been a lot of explaining to do. Buddy was happy because his dad came right on time. "Thanks anyway God," Buddy whispered into the sky before getting in the car.

"Special occasion Dad?" Styles watched Hershey and Conoga make faces and finger gestures through the back window of the car. Buddy thanked God once more and reminded Him that he was still waiting for his muscles.

"Yep. Your mom thinks I should take her out to dinner and you all tag along." Mr. Fieldwest kept his eyes on the road.

"Sounds good to me." "Me too," Buddy added.

It was a glorious day. The family went to Charlie's for dinner. The large crowded restaurant was filled with several unfamiliar faces. The atmosphere was friendly and lively. Mr. Fieldwest was dressed in his work clothes. His tie seemed like it had not been adjusted for hours. Mrs. Fieldwest didn't mind. She was happy just to have everyone together. Styles and Buddy wore the jeans and dress shirt that Mrs. Fieldwest had laid out for them. Hershey and Conoga started right in on them when they got off the bus. Styles convinced Buddy that making mom happy was the sacrifice they had to make. Buddy agreed. "Does that mean I'll get my muscles sooner?" "If God is pleased, yes." It was a good thing Mr. Fieldwest picked them up from school. Hershey and Conoga would have destroyed those clothes!

"Can I take your order?" The very young waiter stood near Mrs. Fieldwest. She prompted Mr. Fieldwest and the boys to place their order.

After the orders, the young waiter bounced away. Minutes later he returned with four glasses of ice water.

"Your order will be ready shortly."

"Young man," Mrs. Fieldwest rose from her seat. She walked with the young man a few steps. "Today is my husband's birthday. Do you have anything special that you do here? I would have called earlier but I wanted it to be a total surprise." She stopped walking. The young waiter smiled, "Yes we do. I'll have someone come over after you've had your dinner."

Mrs. Fieldwest returned to her table. Dinner was wonderful. Mr. Fieldwest was indeed surprised.

"It's too late now. It's so late."

"Mrs. Fieldwest, I have your information. Would you like to speak with Mr. Fieldwest's attending physician?" The crisp voice waited. She knew all too well the feeling one gets when they are about to hear tragic news. She would give Mrs. Fieldwest some time. She waited a couple of minutes more.

"That'll be fine. I'm sorry to be such a bother. Yes, I'd like to speak to the attending physician."

Styles knew that this was when his mom came to the school. On the day she came, he tried to think of anything except for something terribly wrong with his father. He never prepared himself for losing his mom or dad. On the day he sat in the office, he always hoped that his mom finally figured out that he and Buddy were getting jumped and slapped and lunch money taken from them and all kinds of stuff happening to them every day before and after school. He sat and listened and hoped.

"Dad had a terrible stroke. The doctors don't know yet. He was taken to the hospital a few hours ago. The hospital called me at home. I was shaken. I haven't even gone to see him. I just couldn't. I came to see you first. I didn't send for Buddy. It would rip him apart. It was ripping Styles but somebody had to be strong. He knew it was better it be told to him, the oldest son. Mrs. Fieldwest watched Styles slump in the chair. It was all too much too soon. He had to be strong he reminded himself. She promised to be strong. He suddenly appeared thinner. His eyes followed the shadow of the bird outside of the large window. He looked around for the clock. He wasn't sure about the time.

"Mom you're beautiful. You know that?" He didn't know what else to say. "How bad off is Dad? Really."

"Very from what I gathered from the doctor. I can't do it Styles. I just-"

"Mom, we'll be fine. You're beautiful and I better get going, if I'm going to Halley's next year. I better get going." Mrs. Fieldwest smiled and cried. She couldn't decide which were tears of joy and which were tears of pain. Styles moved slowly out of the conference room. He told himself over and over again that it was Wednesday and dad always came to pick them up on Wednesday to go have a burger at Scuds.

Styles patted his mom on her back. The tears streamed down his face. They felt good because no one had seen him cry. No one. Mrs. Fieldwest was so wrapped up in her own grief; she didn't know that Styles was crying. He thought about Buddy and his muscles and he thought about the Wallace children. He had given up all hope on both. He didn't know if he could make it to Halley High School. But he did. Some way somehow, he did. Mrs. Fieldwest gathered her composure once more and pressed on with her story.

"Mrs. Stems watched Styles from the Main Office window. She was anxious to know about Newton. She'd ask Styles later. "It couldn't be too bad," she thought. "She's not taking the boys home."

Mrs. Fieldwest sat in the large conference room gathering her thoughts. She knew she wouldn't have to tell Buddy, because Styles would make sure he understood the situation.

The large conference door opened slowly. The office was completely empty. Mrs. Fieldwest closed the door behind her. When she heard the click, she walked away from the Main Office door. At three o'clock, she walked into her empty home. The front room was still a mess.

"I need to get myself together. Help me God." "Where's Dad Styles?"

"I don't think he's coming today."

"Why'd he not tell us that this morning?" Buddy looked about for Hershey, Conoga and Monroe. As soon as they see we're walking, they'll come Buddy thought.

"He's not going to be coming for a while." Styles looked around too for the Wallace children. Sure enough, there was Hershey leading the small clan. He didn't feel like running today. His mind was clouded. Buddy worried when Styles didn't run so he didn't run. He did make a quick check to see if maybe God had given Styles the muscles. That would have been just fine so long as somebody other than Hershey and Conoga got them. But He hadn't because Styles was still skinny. Buddy wasn't bulging either. Hershey and Conoga closed the space on them. Styles still didn't run so Buddy didn't either. Seconds later, they just took the daily beating from Hershey and Conoga while Monroe watched. Styles couldn't feel the pain. His heart ached. Buddy wondered why they hadn't run.

"What's wrong Styles? We just let them beat the living day lights out of us almost. Something is wrong." Buddy waited and watched Styles little chest go up and down. One would have thought he had muscles from God the way he took those licks from Hershey. Hershey, himself got scared and gave up. "What's going on," Buddy shouted. He knew he had to tell Buddy before they got home. He needed to prepare them for the worst.

Styles and Buddy got home later than usual. Mrs. Fieldwest didn't worry. She figured he was trying to explain things to Buddy. She hoped the two-year gap between their ages worked in her favor of depending on Styles to explain the situation to Buddy. It did. When the boys walked in the door, the look on their mom's face confirmed the deadly reality. Theodore Newton Fieldwest didn't get better.

Three weeks after the funeral, Mrs. Fieldwest cracked under the pressure. The start of the new school year was the continuation of Styles and Buddy being bullied by the Wallace children. It seemed like a lot more.

Styles thought he heard the front door. He rose to check the window leading to the front door. It was just a bird or something. He thought Buddy should be home by now.

* * * * *

Meanwhile Buddy was in Aunt Clara Jean's neighborhood. He wanted to visit Safety. He had the coach drop him off two blocks from where Safety lives. He knew his mom would worry but he had to know. He walked the two blocks hoping not to run into Hershey, Conoga and Monroe. They'd kill him for sure. One thing he and Styles never did was leave the other alone. It was potentially dangerous. Him skipping a grade was the best thing to do. He was sad his father never saw it actually take place. He felt a tear cloud up in the corner of his left eye. It would be okay to cry now. Who would know? Had it been a year or more? He tried to remember. He really couldn't because when it happened, he tried hard to forget. He looked around to see the streets were empty and he let the tears flow. He would hurry since it was a school night.

Styles checked the clock that hung on the wall behind the couch. He worried about Buddy but he didn't want his mom to notice the time. He rubbed her back and she started to speak again in a low voice. He knew it was a lot but she had to get it off her heart. It was a healthy thing to do. He wiped his eyes quickly and continued to listen patting her on her shoulders at the breaking moments. He thought about one of those breaking moments while at the same time watching for Buddy and listening to his mom.

One Sunday morning Mrs. Fieldwest walked into the front room. The scattered materials made her shiver. She stood in the center of the room completely dressed in her church attire. She was beautiful in her baby blue calf-length two-piece outfit. Her hair was pinned neatly in a southern bun. The small fake rubies sparkled in the mid-morning sunlight. "I have to take the boys to see their father." The rubies seemed to have lost their shine.

The warm kitchen door swung open to see Styles standing in the front. He didn't say a word. Buddy followed seconds later. "Mom you are so pretty today. But you know today is Saturday, right? I have a game I think." Styles wore a pair of clean jeans. His short haircut complimented his handsome eyes. He was lean but not as skinny as she remembered. Buddy wore his baseball outfit. His heart was heavy but he decided he'd better not quit. His dad wouldn't be pleased at all. Styles wore a painful expression but he, like Buddy, knew he'd better support Buddy and his playing baseball. His heart glowed with enthusiasm for Buddy's bravery but his face was paled with grief. Mrs. Fieldwest tried all she could to stand strong.

"Your father," she literally whispered, "he's not coming back Styles. He's not coming back. Is he? I'm so scared and I really need you." She cried while Buddy and Styles hugged her at the waist. She smelled pretty with perfume. She thought she was going to see him. That made it all hurt more.

Buddy stepped in front of Safety's gate. He wasn't there. Maybe he went for a walk with his owner Buddy thought. He didn't see a chain or crumbs of food. Nothing. He didn't go inside the gate. He knew it was getting late and he'd have to run home. He just wanted to see Safety for a little bit. He took the hotdog out of his pants' pocket and left it in the corner just outside the gate. He hoped it would still be there on tomorrow. He wished his mom would have to work late. He didn't mind because he wanted to see Safety. He hung around the gate for a few more minutes then started the jog home.

Styles and Mrs. Fieldwest managed to get things out in the open, cry, share a few hugs and put things back to the terrible normal by the time Buddy got home. Dinner was bland but Buddy was so anxious he didn't complain.

"Hey Styles, I went to see Safety today. He wasn't there. You think we'll have to walk to Aunt Clara Jean's tomorrow?" Buddy knew Styles wasn't going to answer. He really didn't mind. Sleep came fast.

Buddy was anxious all day at school. He readily gave up his lunch money to Hershey who took it with shaking hands. Styles followed watching Conoga's hands shake. They were both focused during class and almost ran out of the door when the bell rang. They didn't look too far for Hershey, Conoga and Monroe. They walked fast to keep the gap between them. Buddy wanted to get to Safety's gate. He almost had to drag Styles. They made it! There stood Safety on the top step barking louder than usual Buddy thought. Styles stood at the bottom steps waiting for Buddy to finish petting and praising Safety.

"Styles can you see if the hotdog is still in the corner to your left? I hid it there yesterday after practice." Styles obediently stepped outside the gate and looked for the hotdog. Seconds later he held it in the air. Buddy handed it to Safety who turned his head. Buddy tried a few more times and gave up. He rubbed Safety for a few more minutes thanking him for keeping them safe. Styles motioned for him to get going. It was getting late.

"Thanks Safety," he said and closed the gate.

Aunt Clara Jean had made some pot roast. Buddy was so happy and so hungry. He wasn't frustrated like before.

Safety was the best thing going for him. He was so excited he literally asked Aunt Clara Jean if he could eat in the forbidden room. He felt that brave and equally good. She nodded but Buddy could feel that she didn't whole-heartedly agree to allow him to eat in the forbidden room. In a way she accepted it as progress for the boys. They had been through so much the past years.

He didn't like the tension it would create and but he wanted to try to be comfortable. He gathered his meal and headed for the forbidden room. He wished Styles would sit with him. By reflexes or perhaps pure fear of what might get ruined Aunt Clara Jean followed. Buddy chuckled almost out loud. His heart pattered at the sound of Aunt Clara Jean's crisp duster as she walked practically on the back of his feet. He had to take his time as to not spill the pot roast soup on the antique carpet. He laughed again. Seconds before entering into the room Aunt Clara Jean cut in front of Buddy. She acted as if she had to be the first to enter into the forbidden room. Buddy laughed again. It had been a really good day for him.

Buddy went for a second helping of lunch. It seemed to be more savory than the first or was it because he was sitting in the forbidden room. He looked up at the old clock hanging on the wall. "Mom should be here soon," he said anxiously. "I wonder what Styles thinks of Safety."

He must have been tired from excitement. He went into a deep sleep. First, he dreamt about the day of the funeral. Then he dreamt about the times that he'd begged his mom to let them walk home. One afternoon when his mom picked them up, he started in on his begging. He had choices. He could tell her the Wallace boys were pressuring them. He could say that they were old enough and responsible. He could just sneak home and not tell. The ride home that day reminded him of the ride home the day of the funeral. Styles sat at the window behind the driver's seat. Buddy stared out of all of the windows. He wanted so badly to plead with his mom and tell her the truth but Styles had said no, no, no. Although Styles wasn't talking. Buddy knew he still meant no don't tell. He just wanted to ask his mom to please let them just come straight home. He had asked right before school started that year.

"It is just too dangerous Buddy. I just don't feel right about all of this. It's just too much at once. I want to but I can't. I could never forgive myself if something happened to you while I'm at work and there's no adult supervision. I just can't. Now if your-" She nearly burst into tears. Buddy felt really bad. He wished he hadn't asked. He and Styles were "stuck." The Wallace children bothered them daily. Buddy prayed every night for muscles. After the death of his father, he prayed twice daily. God still hadn't sent any muscles. The situation was hopeless.

Two years later and the struggle continued. "I need some help. We need some help. Styles won't talk, mom doesn't understand, and I don't know what to do," Buddy reminded God. He hoped he heard him this time.

But then he met Safety. He'd never thought of Safety as his muscles against the Wallace children. Aunt Clara Jean and Buddy continued to listen to Styles.

Buddy knew Styles was right about Safety. He didn't tell Styles the whole story about Safety's chain not being there and the fact that no one seemed to ever be at home or hear him do all that loud barking. Also, it seemed like only Hershey, Conoga and Monroe were afraid of Safety. Why had he never bitten them? Safety is a big dog. The first day Buddy went inside the gate, he was scared but he had no choice really. Either way they were going to be hurt; a bite from the dog, or a punch from Hershey. Pain was inevitable on both sides. Buddy followed his heart and slipped inside the gate. Styles followed. It was a promised miracle now that Buddy looked back on it. Safety's bark rang throughout the neighborhood but no one complained. He tried to remember the day God intervened. He wasn't sure. He thought about one Friday night when his mom had worked late. She came to pick them up around eight. Buddy was tired but he would take some time to talk to God. Again.

Mrs. Fieldwest parked the car in front of the apartment complex. She watched her boys, who were now age 13 and 15, file into the apartment. Buddy was glad he ate a second helping at Aunt Clara Jean's. The dark apartment didn't smell of baked potatoes, pot roast, cornbread and apple pie.

"Do you boys have homework?" Buddy watched his mom walk slowly into the apartment while asking her question.

"No homework tonight mom. It's Friday. Are you going to my game tomorrow?" Buddy knew she'd have to work. He still waited for an answer.

"No sweetie. Mom has to work tomorrow. Full day," she added quickly. Mrs. Fieldwest felt her heart in her throat. It had been months since she'd attended one of Buddy's games. She knew Newton wouldn't like the fact that no one showed for Buddy's games. He was so heart set on his son becoming a star as he called it that he nearly demanded the family support him. That was before, thought Mrs. Fieldwest. She wanted to cry right then but what good would it do? She held back her tears for later.

Buddy stared in the mirror at his fragile frame. He wished for the moment that he could be as big as Hershey and as tough as Conoga. He envisioned himself hitting Hershey and Conoga and just pushing Monroe around a little. He would feel brave. He and Styles would be able to walk home by themselves or to Aunt Clara Jean's and no one would bother them. He was the younger brother and his mother would be proud of him. He was already two whole inches taller than Styles and weighed six pounds more. Hershey's not that big Buddy thought. But he is tough, he added.

He flexed the underdeveloped muscles while standing in the mirror. "God, I have got to get those muscles. We're going to get beat to pulps!" Now everyday of the week, they were being harassed. Wednesdays were out because mom worked and Mr. Fieldwest passed on. Thursdays were out because mom worked over time. And every morning was out because mom worked every day and there was no more dad.

"God, I don't want to say I'm tired but I am. I can't concentrate in school. I'm hungry because I have no lunch. I'm scared. Styles isn't growing or talking. So, I have no direction. Look at my calendar." Buddy walked back into his room and pulled the calendar from under his bed. "I started this prayer when I was in seventh grade. I mean really praying and trusting. I am 13 years old and I'm still getting beat up by two older, bigger guys who have nothing else to do. My dad's gone. My mom's working all the time. Styles won't talk and I can't take it anymore." He felt the tears rush down his face. He didn't want to cry because he thought it was girly. He looked around the room. He placed the calendar back under the bed after marking off another day. Tomorrow was Saturday. Yes, mom had to work overtime and yes it would be another deadly walk to their aunt's house. Nonetheless, Buddy prayed to God before sleep took him through the night.

* * * * *

The morning was dim. Buddy rustled the covers before getting up completely. He saw that Styles was not in his bed. Buddy raced downstairs. Styles never got up before him. Something was wrong. He met his mom in the kitchen. Before he could speak, he saw Styles walk past the kitchen door. He was completely dressed.

"Are you going to my game Styles?" Styles knew he had to be there. He feared the Wallaces would be there too for the strangest reasons.

"Styles." Buddy waited for him to stop. "Are you going to my game today?" Styles made no response but Buddy knew he'd be there. He was always there.

"He'll be there sweetie. He's always there." Mrs. Fieldwest tried to hold back her tears. She felt terrible about not making Buddy's games. She used to go to all of his baseball games. She choked thinking about the fact that she barely made four games in the past year.

"It's okay mom. I'll tell you about it when I get home." Buddy knew Hershey would bother them if Mrs. Fieldwest didn't go. He sighed and went upstairs to dress for the game. Styles and Buddy took the city bus to Denvers Park.

At the end of the game Buddy and Styles met up to walk home. Hershey, Conoga and Monroe just appeared.

"Not now guys please. It's Saturday. Styles what do you want us to do? I just played a game and I just don't feel like running home." Buddy didn't expect for Styles to answer.

"Hey girls. Where's your dog?"

The bark from Safety sent the Wallace children to Baly's Corner Store.

Styles and Buddy stood with their mouth opened.

"It's only a miracle Styles. It is!"

CHAPTER SEVEN

The start of another school year sparked Styles a little. He was a senior at age sixteen. He took extra classes during the school year and additional classes during summer break. He finally opened the academic closeness between him and Buddy.

"I'm proud of you Styles." Buddy patted him on the back. Styles grunted. Buddy wondered how Styles made it through the other part of the school year without talking much. He tried to remember the conversations they had before he got his muscles. The day at Aunt Clara Jean's he recalled quickly.

The hallway filled with new faces.

"You're a senior baby. I know you'll do well. I have faith in you. I'm really going to do better. I promise." Styles didn't smile. He hugged his mom and waited for Buddy to walk alongside him. Buddy thought of the months before his dad's death. They were fun and Styles and his mom were always a part of them. Although he missed his dad very much, he was glad to know his mom was happily seeing Mr. Orleans Cradle and Styles was talking and successfully stretching the space between their grade levels and God had finally given him some muscles. Buddy smiled on his way to class.

Mrs. Fieldwest walked them each to their class. Buddy to Language Arts and Styles to Math.

"Mom, you don't have to pick us up today."

"Should I ask why not? I remember just months ago you begged me to pick you up, or let you walk home. What happened?" Mrs. Fieldwest smiled. Buddy hugged her. "Is Mr. Orleans coming with us to Scuds on Wednesday?" She was caught by surprise. She wondered how he knew.

"Styles told me. It's okay mom. We want you to be happy. Mr. Orleans is a nice man. And if he makes you happy, we're happy." She relaxed hearing those words from her youngest son. She didn't think she let on that they were "seeing" each other. She was sure to talk to Styles more about it later. She watched Buddy take his seat in his Language Arts class. Many of the students had not arrived. They still had time. She was glad she came. It made her feel better than she had in the last few months, years even. Buddy had grown into a handsome fourteen-year-old junior. She was so proud of him. She saw Styles walking to his math class. She wanted to shout his name but it would probably embarrass him. Instead, she trotted to catch up with him. Styles smelled her perfume and slowed his pace. He knew, right away, she was trying to catch him. She could have yelled his name. It wouldn't have embarrassed him at all. Although the second bell was about to ring, he still wanted to hear what she had to say.

"Styles." He stopped to look at her.

"Styles, I want you to know I'm sorry about everything. I wish your-" She stopped. She should've known the boys were having a trying year. She should have recognized that they weren't eating lunch. She should have known they felt unsafe.

She should have known. Too much time had passed and she didn't know. "It's all my fault. I should've known. I'm their mother!" She was sure not to let her face express her thoughts.

But Styles already knew.

"Mom, please don't be hard on yourself. The person, the Spirit, if you will, that did help us was the right choice. You did your best and I'm happy. Dad did his best and I'm grateful.

God did it all because He loves us." Styles stepped aside to let one of his classmates by. "You're beautiful mom. That'll never change. Buddy wanted muscles from God. I never told you before because it was between him and God. He trusted God for a long time, mom. He was strong like you wouldn't believe." Styles' voice was low. Mrs. Fieldwest held on to every word. Styles stopped talking after the sudden death of Theodore Newton Fieldwest, the greatest thing in his life. Mrs. Fieldwest could have stood outside of Styles' class all day listening to him speak. "Buddy wanted those muscles mom. He waited and waited because Dad always told us to, when we were kids, to wait on God and don't complain. Buddy did good mom. It's been three years and it's over." Styles wanted to cry but too many students began to fill the hallways. This cry would be tears of joy.

"Styles I'm getting married. I didn't talk to Buddy."

"I know mom. Mr. Orleans to you is like Safety is to Buddy." Styles remembered what Orleans Cradle asked him.

"Please don't tell your mom I asked you this until after we get married. I asked you for your approval because you are a bright young fellow." Styles prayed that night and God told him in his dream that everything was going to be alright. He would have a new father to see after him, Buddy, and his mom.

But especially his mom.

"But what about you Styles? What do you get?" Mrs. Fieldwest knew the last bell was about to ring, but this moment was important. She really wanted to know.

"You and Buddy. I got you and Buddy. And soon I'll have Mr. Orleans. I was angry with God at first. Buddy kept praying for those muscles. You did your very best to keep things under control. I backed out. I wasn't there for you and Buddy because I was angry. Hershey and Conoga beat us up everyday and I never told you because I wanted God to give Buddy those muscles and he'd beat up the Wallace boys. Or worse mom Buddy wouldn't get the muscles and we'd get beat up everyday and I'd have a greater excuse to be angry with God."

The sound of the last bell sent Mrs. Fieldwest and Styles in an embrace. Hundreds of children hurried through the hallways. They stepped around them as they walked and the few who stepped into the Calculus II class. Mrs. Fieldwest wiped her tears and a few of Styles'.

"Mom."

"Yes sweetie."

"Buddy has his muscles from God."

"He does. I didn't see any muscles on that boy." Mrs. Fieldwest couldn't understand what Styles was referring to when he spoke about Buddy and praying for muscles. She was so horrified about all those beatings that she broke down with guilt listening to Styles talk.

"Safety."

"Who?"

"The way God works is like my Calculus II class. It'll take a long time to get it if you don't understand and open your mind to the logic." Mrs. Fieldwest always knew Styles was a born genius.

"Safety?"
Meanwhile Buddy heard clearly Safety's bark.
God had finally come through with some muscles.

After The Miracle

"Strike two!" The empire swept a little dust as the words echoed through his baseball mask. Boderrick (Buddy) Newton Fieldwest didn't sweat at the hearty sound of strike two. He made a tighter grip on the baseball bat and concentrated on happy thoughts. The stout five foot eleven inch, two hundred ten pound twenty-year-old took his calm stance at the home plate. He took a deep breath and repeated, "I can do all things through Christ which strengthens me." He smiled and looked for his mother and brother in the crowd. In a few seconds, he spotted Mrs. Cradle and his brother Styles.

"I see you sweetie," yelled Mrs. Cradle from the stands. She waved her hands wildly. Styles waved too and yelled something. Buddy didn't hear him.

Although Styles was only five feet seven and weighed around one hundred sixty pounds, Buddy still loved him the same. He was his big brother and that would never change. Mr. Orleans Cradle was unable to make Buddy's game this time due to work conflicts. Buddy was fine with it. Mr. Orleans Cradle turned out to be an excellent stepfather. Buddy and Styles missed their own father but loved Mr. Orleans Cradle with all of their heart.

While concentrating on the next pitch, Buddy tried not to think of his father, Theodore Newton Fieldwest. Times had been really hard for him, Styles, and his mother, but God made several ways for them. The pitch!

Buddy cracked the ball with great strength, sending it well into the back rows of the stands. The roaring of the crowd took him back to the time he first laid eyes on the professional baseball field. The tears rolled down his mother's cheeks like rain. She could feel his thoughts as the ball flew past Styles' head. Buddy could feel his mom's sincere congratulations for his success while at the same time wished that his father was there to celebrate. The ball continued to find an escape route in the stands. Buddy ran to first base. He ran to second base with strong enthusiasm and less effort. Third base was even easier. He had time to wave to his mom and brother again. Then he ran to home plate.

Home. Home was a thousand miles away right now and Buddy was very happy to know that he would not be returning to his home in Camden, New Jersey. He was so very happy to not have to run to save his life, almost. He took some time to thank God for his real muscles. He thanked God for the strength not only to play baseball, but also to know that God cares. Buddy placed his foot on home plate. This home run marked the twenty-second home run for the season. Boderrick Newton Fieldwest was really making a name for himself. He again searched the stands to find his mother and brother. Again, his mother waved wildly and Styles yelled something else Buddy couldn't hear. They were jumping and yelling. It was a great day in Chicago, Illinois.

God, Where Are My Muscles?

From a parent's perspective

Children, remember that God loves you more than you'll ever realize. He doesn't want you to be hurt, sad, or lonely. But He does want you to be patient, loving, and caring. Buddy loved God and he trusted Him to help him. He never gave up and God was there for Him. Although Safety probably wasn't Buddy's idea of "muscles", God still gave him want he needed. He still gave him something to keep Hershey, Conoga and Monroe from bothering him and his brother. Trust in God and know that He wants us to make it. No matter what.

A Note From The Author

I love children. Spending time with my own and sometimes others are one of my favorite past times. I know how it feels to be different or unpopular. I was like that when I was in grade school. I was different so other children picked on me. I, like Buddy and Styles, didn't let my parents know. What helped me was my parents' love for me and knowing that God loves me too.

God, Where Are My Muscles? is a traditional setting of many of our children today. Bullying is a silent destroyer of healthy self-esteem. Sadly, it takes place in our schools and in our communities. Thus, we as adults need to be aware. Don't think it doesn't exist. It's there in many fashions. Sometimes children won't come right out and tell you. They feel they might get teased for tattling as well.

Buddy and Styles didn't tell their parents and that wasn't good. I have my own children. My son was ten years old at the time and he felt like he was just to small to be great. too small. I was almost certain that he'd get picked on in school. He wanted muscles then and he wants them now. Tell your children it's okay to let someone know. Also tell them that the solution to a problem may not always require any physical intervention on their part. Safety is a dog and he was as much help as it would have been for Buddy to have muscles to beat up Hershey and Conoga.

Remember, we can all be a parent to a child. Let that child know that God loves him/her and He will always be their muscle as they try to make it in today's world.

Osiander Rose

ABOUT THE AUTHOR

Osiander Rose is a dynamic writer. She has grown closer in and to Christ. She writes about her understanding of God's perfect plan in such a way that all levels of Christians can understand. Take time to also read Preaching to the Tenth Pew, books 1-4 and A Boat in the Desert. We hope you enjoyed *"God, Where Are My Muscles?"* You'd be amazed to know how good God is and how much He truly loves His people.

Osiander Rose is going places and she has a testimony to tell. You'll love her and the words she puts to print.

www.ingramcontent.com/pod-product-compliance
Lightning Source LLC
Chambersburg PA
CBHW060350130626
46553CB00003B/1160